Data Governance Guide for BCBS 239 and DFAST Compliance

Sunil Soares

Information Asset LLC

Harrington Park, NJ

www.information-asset.com

Data Governance Guide for BCBS 239 and DFAST Compliance
Sunil Soares

First Edition

Information Asset LLC
Harrington Park, NJ USA
www. information-asset.com

ISBN: 978-0692713815   Printed by CreateSpace

About Sunil Soares

Sunil Soares is the founder and managing partner of Information Asset, a consulting firm that specializes in data governance. Prior to this role, Sunil was the director of information governance at IBM and worked with clients across six continents and multiple industries.

Sunil is the author of several books on data governance, including *The IBM Data Governance Unified Process*, *Selling Information Governance to the Business: Best Practices by Industry and Job Function*, *Big Data Governance*, *IBM InfoSphere: A Platform for Big Data Governance and Process Data Governance*, *Data Governance Tools*, and *The Chief Data Officer Handbook for Data Governance*.

Prior to joining IBM, Sunil consulted with major financial institutions at the Financial Services Strategy Consulting Practice of Booz Allen & Hamilton in New York. Sunil lives in New Jersey and holds an MBA in Finance and Marketing from the University of Chicago Booth School of Business.

Contents

Preface

BCBS and DFAST compliance is the major systemic issue facing financial institutions in the post–Great Recession landscape. With the guidelines for both global and domestic compliance evolving rapidly, the imperative to actively engage on BCBS and DFAST obligations is increasing as the first compliance deadlines arrive.

At the core of those obligations is data governance: a set of best practices that optimize, secure, and leverage information as an enterprise asset by aligning the objectives of multiple functions.

This book provides both a concise explanation of how data governance best practices dovetail with BCBS and DFAST compliance requirements and outlines a high-level blueprint for creating a data governance plan, infrastructure, and processes aligned with those compliance goals.

The book consists of the following sections:

1. *The Regulatory Imperative for Data Governance in Financial Services*

   How and why U.S. and global regulatory requirements drive the need for data governance in the financial services industry

2. *Operationalizing Data Governance*

   An overview of the 16-step, end-to-end approach for operationalizing data governance

3. *Data Governance Playbook*

   Establishing the framework for data policies, standards, and processes

4. *Data Categories*

   Creating appropriate level 1, 2, and 3 data categories and assigning ownership

5. *Data Ownership*

   An overview of the roles and responsibilities required to drive data ownership on an organization-wide basis

6. *Critical Data Elements*

   Deriving, populating, and working with critical data elements

7. *Data Quality*

   Establishing data-quality dimensions, rules, and scorecards and remediating data issues

8. *Analytical Models and End User Computing*

   Organizing and governing inventories of analytical models and end user computing applications

9. *Data Lineage*

   An overview of business and technical lineage, why data lineage matters, and establishing data lineage reports

10. *Data Service Level Agreements*

    The properties of data service level agreements and templates for establishing them

11. *Data Sharing Agreements and Data Attestations*

    The properties of data sharing agreements and attestations plus templates for establishing them

12. *Data Governance Dashboards*

    Data governance dashboards, their uses, and how to construct them

13. *Data Governance Audits*

    Establishing enforcement standards, consequences, and remediation activities

Geared toward business users, this book is non-technical and provides an overview of the data governance process for the following roles:

- Chief Financial Officer
- Chief Risk Officer
- Chief Operating Officer
- Chief Information Officer
- Chief Data Officer
- Enterprise Data Management Lead
- Enterprise Information Management Lead
- Data Governance Lead
- Data Steward
- Regulators and Examiners

1

The Regulatory Imperative for Data Governance in Financial Services

Data governance is the formulation of policy to optimize, secure, and leverage information as an enterprise asset by aligning the objectives of multiple functions. By its very nature, data governance boosts cross-departmental cooperation, delivers timely, trustworthy data, and allows all departments to make better decisions.

However, in the financial services sector, data governance has a specific—and crucial—role to ensure that the information in regulatory reports is trustworthy. In the aftermath of the global financial crisis, regulators responded with heightened efforts to ensure that banks had sufficient capital to withstand economic shocks.

BCBS 239

BCBS 239 is industry shorthand for the Basel Committee on Banking Supervision's *Principles for Effective Risk Data Aggregation and Risk Reporting*, released in January 2013. The Basel Committee on Banking Supervision (BCBS), which is the major international source for regulation and supervision of banks, issues guidelines and standards that, while not backed by legal consequences, are internationally accepted as best practices throughout the financial industry. The U.S. Federal Reserve has adopted many of the Basel principles in its regulations.

BCBS 239 outlines 14 principles of risk management and requires a bank to comply with the standards attached to those principles within three years of its designation as a global, systemically important bank (G-SIB) or as a domestic, systemically important bank (D-SIB). G-SIBs are identified by the Financial Stability Board (FSB) and are subject to higher loss absorbency requirements, regular assessments of their resolvability, and higher supervisory expectations. A bank that is not a G-SIB can still qualify as a domestic, systemically important bank according to several lists maintained and released by the U.S. Federal Reserve, the European Union, or other governing bodies. D-SIB banks must comply with more stringent stress test requirements, higher capital requirements, and increased supervision standards.

These regulations also apply to certain systemically important financial institutions (SIFIs), which include non-banking financial institutions such as insurance companies. Under Section 113 of the U.S. Dodd-Frank Wall Street Reform and Consumer Protection Act ("Dodd-Frank Act"), the Financial Stability Oversight Council (FSOC) is authorized to determine that a nonbank financial company's material financial distress—or the nature, scope, size, scale, concentration, interconnectedness, or mix of its activities—could pose a threat to U.S. financial stability.[1] The FSOC has a statutory mandate to identify risks and respond to emerging threats to financial stability in the United States. The FSOC is chaired by the Secretary of the U.S. Treasury and includes representatives from the Federal Reserve and other federal and state regulatory bodies.

DFAST

Section 165(i)(2) of the Dodd-Frank Act requires national banks and federal savings associations with total consolidated assets of more than $10 billion to conduct annual stress tests. The results of the company-run stress tests provide the Office of the Comptroller of the Currency (OCC) with forward-looking information used in bank supervision and assist the agency in assessing the company's risk profile and capital adequacy.

CCAR

One of the principal functions of the Federal Reserve is to regulate and supervise financial institutions, including bank holding companies (BHCs), savings and loan holding companies, state member banks, and systemically important nonbank financial institutions. One of the key cross-firm programs is an annual assessment by the Federal Reserve of whether BHCs with $50 billion or more in total consolidated assets have

---

[1] https://www.treasury.gov/initiatives/fsoc/designations/Pages/default.aspx

effective capital adequacy processes and sufficient capital to absorb losses during stressful conditions, while meeting obligations to creditors and counterparties and continuing to serve as credit intermediaries. This annual assessment includes two related programs[2]:

- The *Comprehensive Capital Analysis and Review (CCAR)* evaluates a BHC's capital adequacy, capital adequacy process, and planned capital distributions, such as dividend payments and common stock repurchases. As part of CCAR, the Federal Reserve evaluates whether BHCs have sufficient capital to continue operations throughout times of economic and financial market stress and whether they have robust, forward-looking capital-planning processes that account for their unique risks. If the Federal Reserve objects to a BHC's capital plan, the BHC may not make any capital distribution unless the Federal Reserve indicates in writing that it does not object to the distribution.

- *Dodd-Frank Act supervisory stress testing* is a forward-looking quantitative evaluation of the impact of stressful economic and financial market conditions on BHC capital. This program serves to inform these financial companies, as well as the general public, how the institutions' capital ratios might change during a hypothetical set of adverse economic conditions as designed by the Federal Reserve. In addition to the annual supervisory stress test conducted by the Federal Reserve, each BHC is required to conduct annual company-run stress tests under the same supervisory scenarios and to conduct a mid-cycle stress test under company-developed scenarios.

Data Governance Requirements Are Broadly Similar Across BCBS 239 and DFAST and Across Supervisory Agencies

The BCBS Regulatory Consistency Assessment Programme (RCAP) found that the risk-based capital requirements in the United States are largely compliant with the minimum standards agreed upon under the

---

[2] Board of Governors of the Federal Reserve System, Dodd-Frank Act Stress Test 2015: Supervisory Stress Test Methodology and Results, March 2015, http://www.federalreserve.gov/newsevents/press/bcreg/bcreg20150305a1.pdf

Basel framework.[3] Because BCBS 239 and DFAST have similar data collection requirements, this book treats these regulations interchangeably from a data governance perspective.

In the United States, three federal agencies—the Federal Reserve, the Office of the Comptroller of the Currency (OCC), and the Federal Deposit Insurance Corporation (FDIC)—have regulatory authority over bank supervision and stress testing at large financial institutions. While the actual forms and reports vary, there is a remarkable degree of similarity in the actual data being collected. As a result, this book treats these bodies interchangeably from a data governance perspective.

The Role of Data Governance

Regulators rely on the trustworthiness of information in regulatory reports. If these reports contain inaccuracies, then it is likely that regulators may make incorrect decisions. The traditional data governance disciplines of data ownership, metadata management, data quality management, and model governance also apply in this area. It is just that the stakes are high and there is a significant regulatory component. A strong data governance strategy is a pivotal part of the landscape for BCBS 239 and DFAST compliance.

Summary

- While data governance is good business practice in every industry, it is crucial in financial services in order to comply with BCBS 239 and DFAST regulatory requirements.

- BCBS 239 standards apply to G-SIBs and D-SIBs and have been largely adopted by the U.S. Federal Reserve.

- DFAST is a federally mandated stress test for U.S. banks with assets over $10 billion.

---

[3] Basel Committee on Banking Supervision, Regulatory Consistency Assessment Programme (RCAP), Assessment of Basel III regulations–United States of America, December 2014, http://www.bis.org/bcbs/publ/d301.pdf

2

Operationalizing Data Governance

Operationalizing data governance for BCBS 239 and DFAST involves 16 steps, which are shown in Figure 2.1. Organizations may adopt a different sequence depending on their specific requirements.

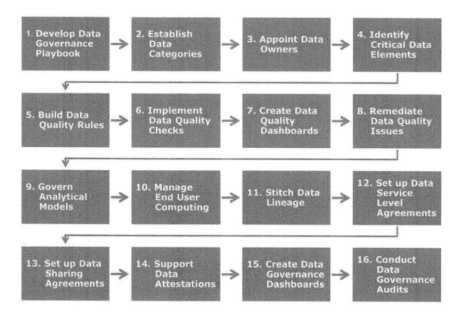

Figure 2.1: An end-to-end approach to operationalizing data governance

1. Develop Data Governance Playbook

The first step is to develop a data governance playbook with policies, standards, and processes. Data policies establish high-level guidance to be implemented by standards. For example, a data ownership policy may be implemented by standards that define the various data governance roles, including lead data steward, business data steward, technical data steward, and executive sponsor. A data quality policy may be implemented by a standard that defines data quality dimensions, such as completeness, conformity, and accuracy. Data quality processes include those for triage and issue resolution.

2. Establish Data Categories

The data governance team needs to collaborate with enterprise data architecture to classify data into categories. For example, an insurance carrier may have multiple data categories including marketing, product, claims, finance, and underwriting. The finance data category may be further subdivided into data categories for chart of accounts and billing. These data categories are a crucial precursor to defining data ownership.

3. Appoint Data Owners

The next step is to define data owners based on the roles in the playbook and the data categories. This approach accommodates the reality that the same business term may have different meanings in separate parts of the business. Taking the insurance example further, the marketing data steward may define "customer" to include prospects, the underwriting data steward may include current policyholders only, and the claims data steward may have an expansive definition that includes witnesses to an accident.

4. Identify Critical Data Elements

This exhaustive 16-step process implies that data governance is a very rigorous exercise. Data stewards should prioritize their efforts by identifying Critical data elements (CDEs) within their respective data categories. CDEs have a major impact on financial reporting, operating performance, or regulatory reporting. For example, a risk data steward in a bank may identify Legal Entity ID as a CDE that supports compliance with BCBS 239.

5. Build Data Quality Rules

Data stewards must build data quality rules for CDEs. For example, a data quality rule may state, "Legal Entity ID must be unique for a given counterparty legal entity."

6. Implement Data Quality Checks

Data stewards, in conjunction with their technical counterparts, should implement data quality checks based on the rules defined earlier. These data quality checks may be scheduled on a regular basis or on demand. Regularly scheduled data quality checks may be implemented in the form of batch Extract Transform Load (ETL) jobs. On-demand data quality checks may be implemented with Structured Query Language (SQL) scripts or out-of-the-box tools.

7. Create Data Quality Dashboards

Data quality dashboards are a useful way to summarize results. These dashboards may roll up results by division, data category, data quality dimension, and data quality rule.

8. Remediate Data Quality Issues

Data governance teams need processes to remediate data issues. These processes must cover the following activities:

- Identify a data issue

- Log a data issue

- Triage a data issue based on criteria such as impact on revenues, cost, or capital allocation

- Assign a data issue

- Investigate a data issue

- Resolve a data issue

9. Govern Analytical Models

Risk models should be governed in a similar manner as CDEs. At a minimum, model governance teams needs to build a model inventory that includes the name of the model, the model owner, input variables, output variables, model methodology, the creation date, and completed or planned validation activities. Ideally, model governance teams should be able to demonstrate model lineage back to CDEs and source data.

10. Manage End User Computing

Organizations typically generate a significant volume of end user computing (EUC) applications in the form of spreadsheets, SAS® datasets, and databases that may be stored on desktops or in Microsoft® SharePoint® repositories. DFAST and BCBS 239 require EUC applications to be governed if they contain analytical models. EUC governance teams need to build an inventory of critical EUCs, which contains the name of the application, the owner, input variables, output variables, and the creation date.

11. Stitch Data Lineage

Financial institutions often have to answer questions from the regulators:

- Where did the data pertaining to a field in this report come from?
- What data quality checks were applied to the source data?
- Who owns the source data?

Organizations need a strong metadata foundation to be able to answer such questions. Once metadata tools have ingested business and technical metadata from a variety of data sources, organizations should be able to address these questions.

12. Set up Data Service Level Agreements

Data Service Level Agreements (SLAs) are intracompany contracts that govern the movement of critical data to support calculations for BCBS 239 and DFAST reports. Data SLAs contain information pertaining to the attributes being shared, whether any of the attributes are CDEs, acceptable thresholds of data quality, and accountability if data quality thresholds are not met.

13. Set up Data Sharing Agreements

Data sharing agreements are intracompany contracts that support data attestation. Data sharing agreements may be chained together with other data sharing agreements and data SLAs to provide a level of comfort to the overall attesting executive that the underlying data is trustworthy.

14. Support Data Attestations

Financial regulations often require a single executive to attest to the veracity of data in key filings. The attesting data executive will require other executives to certify the trustworthiness of data being used in reports. As discussed earlier, the data governance team needs to establish a framework based on data sharing agreements and data SLAs to support attestation to the regulators.

15. Create Data Governance Dashboards

Data governance monitoring involves regular reporting on the level of compliance with data policies, standards, and processes. A data governance dashboard is a useful approach to monitor compliance by relying on peer pressure to improve adherence to data policies, standards, and processes.

16. Conduct Data Governance Audits

Data governance monitoring is a softer approach to ensuring compliance with data policies, standards, and processes. On the other hand, data governance enforcement requires tangible consequences to non-compliance with data policies, standards, and processes. This includes regular audits by business teams, data governance, and the internal audit department.

Summary

- There are 16 core steps to operationalize a data governance program geared to BCBS 239 and DFAST compliance.

- The order of steps and the importance of each step may vary based on each organization's needs and existing data governance structures.

- Data governance is a multi-departmental effort, the initiation of which will encourage overall collaboration across the organization.

3

Data Governance Playbook

The first step in the data governance journey is to build a data governance playbook. A data governance playbook is a guide to allow banks to establish a framework to manage data policies, standards, and processes. These artifacts may be found in many places, including in people's heads or embedded in broader policy manuals. Some organizations document their policies in Microsoft Word® or PowerPoint® and load the documents to SharePoint or an intranet portal. The data governance playbook is the guide that supports the operationalization of the overall program.

Prescribe Terminology for Data Policies

A number of terms—such as policies, standards, processes, guidelines, and principles—are used to describe data decisions. Banks must employ consistent terminology to describe these data decisions. In this book, we use a standard framework of data policies, standards, and processes. We begin this chapter by defining these key terms:

- *Data policies*—These provide a broad framework for how decisions should be made regarding data. Data policies are high-level statements and need more detail before they can be operationalized. Each data policy may be supported by one or more data standards.

- *Data standards*—These provide detailed rules about how to implement data policies. Each data standard may be supported by one or more data processes.

- *Data processes*—These provide special instructions about how to implement data standards.

Data policies, standards, and processes follow a hierarchy as shown in Figure 3.1.

Figure 3.1: The hierarchy of data policies, standards, and processes

As Figure 3.2 shows, data governance is a foundational program that ties together the other enterprise data management (EDM) disciplines.

We discuss each EDM discipline below:

- *Data governance*—The formulation of policy to optimize, secure, and leverage information as an enterprise asset by aligning the objectives of multiple functions

- *Data ownership*—The process of identifying individuals who will be accountable for the trustworthiness of data within their purview

- *Data architecture*—A discipline that sets data standards for data systems as a vision or a model of the eventual interactions between those data systems[1]

---

[1] http://en.wikipedia.org/wiki/Data_architecture

Figure 3.2: The EDM disciplines that contribute to good data governance

- *Data modeling*—The process of establishing data models, which use a set of symbols and text to precisely explain a subset of real information to improve communication within the organization and thereby lead to a more flexible and stable application environment[2]

- *Data integration*—A process that involves combining data from multiple sources to provide new insights to business users

---

[2] *Data Modeling Made Simple, 2nd Edition* (Steve Hoberman, Technics Publications, LLC, 2009).

- *Database management and operations*—The process of managing data repositories

- *Data security and privacy*—The process of avoiding unauthorized access to data

- *Master data management*—The process of establishing a single version of the truth for an organization's critical data entities, such as customers, products, materials, vendors, and chart of accounts

- *Reference data management*—The process of managing static data, such as country codes, state or province codes, and industry classification codes, which may be placed in lookup tables for reference by other applications across the enterprise

- *Data warehousing*—The process of creating a centralized repository of data for reporting and analysis

- *Critical data elements*—Data elements that are determined to be vital to the success of an organization and represent significant regulatory or operational risk

- *Metadata management*—The management of information that describes the characteristics of any data artifact, such as its name, location, criticality, quality, business rules, and relationships to other data artifacts

- *Data quality management*—A discipline that includes methods to measure and improve the quality and integrity of an organization's data

- *Information lifecycle management*—The process and methodology of managing information through its lifecycle, from creation through disposal, including compliance with legal, regulatory, and privacy requirements

- *Content management*—The process of digitizing, collecting, and classifying paper and electronic documents

The key EDM disciplines for BCBS 239 and DFAST compliance are data ownership, data architecture (data categories), critical data elements, metadata management, and data quality management. At the very minimum, the data governance playbook should include policies, standards, and processes to support these EDM disciplines. The remainder of this chapter will review some examples of data policies, standards, and processes.

Data Quality Management Policy

Figure 3.3 shows a hierarchy of policy, standards, and processes for data quality management. The overall data policy, in the highest box, includes within it standards for accountability, critical data elements, and the data quality scorecard. The accountability data standard also encompasses the data issue resolution process.

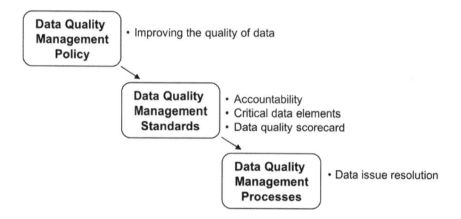

Figure 3.3: The relationship between data quality management policy, standards, and processes

Policy

A sample policy for data quality management used in Figure 3.3 is shown below:

> Data quality management is a discipline that includes the methods to measure and improve the quality and integrity of an organization's data. We must adhere to an enterprise-approved process to manage and improve the quality of business-critical data.

Standards

The data quality management standards that would apply to this policy are as follows:

- *Accountability*—The data governance team must lead the overall data quality program. However, each data owner must assign one or more business data stewards to manage data quality for key systems and data domains. The responsibilities of the data steward include identifying critical data elements, creating business rules for data profiling, and resolving data issues.

- *Critical data elements*—The data steward must identify critical data elements, which will be the focus of the data quality program. Critical data elements must constitute not more than 10 to 15 percent of the total attributes in a data domain or data repository. These critical data elements must be used to create data quality rules that will drive the data quality scorecard. For example, "The value of collateral for secured loans cannot be null or blank" is a data quality rule that relates to the "collateral" critical data element. If secured loans have null collateral, then they will have to be treated as unsecured loans when computing risk-weighted assets.

- *Data quality scorecard*—The data governance team must manage a data quality scorecard to track key metrics by system and data domain. This scorecard must be updated on a monthly basis and will be circulated to key stakeholders.

Process

Finally, the accountability data standard in Figure 3.3 links to the data issue resolution process. This process states that the lead data steward must track data issues in a log that will be circulated to stakeholders on a periodic basis. This log must track the list of data issues, severity, assignee, date assigned, and current status.

Metadata Management Policy

Figure 3.4 shows a sample hierarchy of metadata management policy and standards. The overall metadata management policy refers to the data standards for the business glossary, data stewardship, business rules, and data lineage and impact analysis. No data processes have been defined in this case.

Figure 3.4: A sample hierarchy of metadata management policy and standards

Policy

A sample metadata management policy for Figure 3.4 is shown below:

We must have quality metadata stored within an enterprise metadata repository to manage business terms, technical metadata, business rules, data quality rules, master data rules, reference data, data lineage, and impact analysis.

Standards

The metadata management policy for Figure 3.4 relates to the following metadata management standards:

- *Business glossary*—The data governance team must maintain a business glossary with definitions of key business terms. These business definitions must be created and maintained for critical data elements using organizationally adopted naming and definition standards. The business glossary will also contain a data dictionary with the definitions of column and table names for key data repositories.

- *Data stewardship*—Data owners must assign data stewards to manage business terms and other data artifacts such as business rules.

- *Business rules*—Business rules for critical data elements must be documented and kept up-to-date for each data repository and must be reflected within the business glossary.

- *Data lineage and impact analysis*—The metadata repository must ingest metadata from key systems, including relational databases, data modeling tools, data integration platforms, reports, risk models, and Hadoop®. The lineage of data elements must be documented and should be up-to-date, and impact analysis must also be performed.

Establish Process for Data Policy Changes

Banks must establish a process to manage changes to data policies, standards, and processes. The appropriate body, such as the data governance council, must approve these changes.

Summary

- The data governance playbook is a key artifact that documents policies, standards, and processes to operationalize data governance.

- Data policies are high-level statements and need more detail before they can be operationalized.

- Data standards provide detailed rules on how to implement data policies.

- Data processes provide special instructions on how to implement data standards.

- Each data policy may be supported by one or more data standards. Each data standard may be supported by one or more data processes.

4

Data Categories

Data Categories

Basel Committee on Banking Supervision, Principles for Effective Risk Data Aggregation and Risk Reporting, *January 2013, Principle 2 – Data architecture and IT infrastructure, Paragraph 33*

A bank should establish integrated data taxonomies and architecture across the banking group, which includes information on the characteristics of the data (metadata).

A data category is a logical classification of information to support data governance. Data categories are critical to downstream data governance activities, especially data stewardship. If data categories are not established correctly, it will be difficult to identify data stewards.

Define Level 1 Data Categories in Collaboration with Data Architecture

The data governance and data architecture teams need to collaborate to define the data categories for the enterprise. The initial classification of data categories may be based on an enterprise conceptual model or enterprise logical data model.

The definition of the level 1 data categories is often a tug-of-war between data governance and data architecture. Data architecture may define a data category, but data governance may find it difficult to identify a data owner for that category. For example, **Customer** may not be an appropriate level 1 data category for a large multinational financial services organization because there is no owner for customer data across the enterprise.

Define Level 2 and Lower Data Categories

The next step is to define level 2 and lower data categories. As an example, let's select the annual DFAST 10-50 report that is submitted to the OCC. The OCC DFAST 10-50 report is a company-run stress test that collects detailed data about national banks and federal savings associations with consolidated assets of $10 billion to $50 billion. This data includes quantitative projections of income, losses, assets, liabilities, and capital across a range of macroeconomic scenarios as well as qualitative supporting information on the methodologies and processes used to develop internal projections of capital across scenarios. The OCC DFAST 10-50 report is required to reflect financials as of December 31 and must be submitted by the close of business July 31 of each calendar year, unless that time is extended by the OCC in writing.

The OCC DFAST 10-50 report is organized into the following sections:

    A. Scenario Variables Schedule
    B. Results Schedule
        a. Summary Schedule
        b. Baseline Scenario
            i. Income Statement
            ii. Balance Sheet Statement
        c. Adverse Scenario
            i. Income Statement
            ii. Balance Sheet Statement
        d. Severely Adverse Scenario
            i. Income Statement
            ii. Balance Sheet Statement

The OCC has defined the three scenarios, which were developed in coordination with the Federal Reserve Board and the Federal Deposit Insurance Corporation:[1]

- The *baseline scenario* for the United States is a moderate economic expansion. Real Gross Domestic Product (GDP) grows at an average rate of 2½ percent per year. The unemployment rate declines to 4½ percent, and Consumer Price Index (CPI) inflation rises to 2½ percent at an annual rate before dropping back to about 2 percent. Accompanying the moderate expansion,

---

[1] Office of the Comptroller of the Currency, U.S. Department of the Treasury, *Annual Stress Test Baseline, Adverse, and Severely Adverse Scenarios*, January 28, 2016.

Treasury yields are assumed to rise steadily across the maturity spectrum. Asset prices rise modestly. The baseline scenario for international economic activity and inflation features an expansion in activity, albeit one that proceeds at different rates across countries.

- The *adverse scenario* is characterized by weakening economic activity across all countries included in the scenario. The economic downturn is accompanied by a period of deflation in the United States and in the other countries. In the United States, consumer prices fall about ½ percent over the four quarters of 2016. Reflecting weak economic conditions and deflationary pressures, short-term interest rates in the United States remain near zero over the projection period. Financial conditions tighten for corporations and households during the recession, and asset prices decline in the adverse scenario.

- The *severely adverse* scenario is characterized by a severe global recession, accompanied by a heightened period of corporate financial stress and negative yields for short-term U.S. Treasury securities. Corporate financial conditions are severely stressed, reflecting mounting credit losses, heightened investor risk aversion, and strained market liquidity conditions. The international component of the severely adverse scenario features severe recessions in the euro area, the United Kingdom, and Japan and a mild recession in developing Asia. As a result of acute economic weakness, all foreign economies included in the scenario experience a pronounced decline in consumer prices.

The variables describing economic developments within the United States include:

- *Six measures of economic activity and prices*—Percent changes (at an annual rate) in real and nominal GDP, the unemployment rate of the civilian non-institutional population aged 16 and over, percent changes (at an annual rate) in real and nominal disposable personal income, and the percent change (at an annual rate) in the CPI

- *Four aggregate measures of asset prices or financial conditions*—Indices of house prices, commercial property prices, equity prices, and U.S. stock-market volatility

- *Six measures of interest rates*—The rate on the three-month Treasury bill; the yield on the five-year Treasury bond; the yield on the 10-year Treasury bond; the yield on a 10-year BBB corporate security; the interest rate associated with a conforming, conventional, fixed-rate, 30-year mortgage; and the prime rate

For the variables describing international economic conditions, each scenario includes three variables in four countries or country blocks:

- *The three variables for each country or country block*—The percent change (at an annual rate) in real GDP, the percent change (at an annual rate) in the CPI or local equivalent, and the level of the U.S. dollar/foreign currency exchange rate

- *The four countries or country blocks included*—The euro area (the 19 European Union member states that have adopted the euro as their common currency), the United Kingdom, developing Asia (the nominal GDP-weighted aggregate of China, India, South Korea, Hong Kong SAR, and Taiwan), and Japan

Figure 4.1 shows a subset of the data categories at a financial institution. In this example, the level 1 data category is risk. This category contains multiple level 2 data categories: scenario variables, credit risk, market risk, and operational risk. The scenario variables data category also contains a number of level 3 data categories, by geographic region. Finally, the United States data category is further broken down into three level 4 data categories.

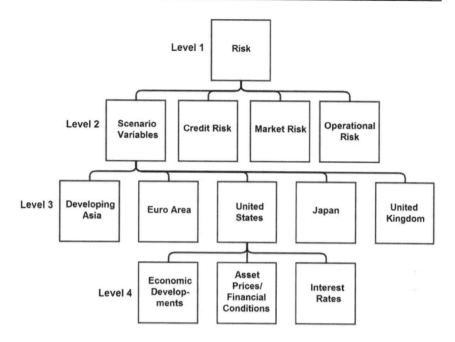

Figure 4.1: A sample hierarchy of data categories used to define variables for DFAST scenarios

Conduct a Sanity Check to Ensure That Each Data Category Has Clearly Defined Ownership

The final step is to ensure that each data category has clearly defined ownership. As we discussed earlier, **Customer** may not be an appropriate level 1 data category for a large multinational financial services organization because there is no owner for customer data across the enterprise. However, as Figure 4.2 demonstrates, **Customer** may be a more appropriate Level 4 data category. In this example, the bank needs to assign a specific owner for customer data within retail banking in Germany due to data privacy laws. Similarly, the bank can easily assign an owner for investment banking customer data within the United States. As a result, even though **Customer** had no owner at level 1, the legal and organizational framework in which the bank operates day to day may make it the best choice to create multiple level 4 data categories for **Customer** across various divisions and regions.

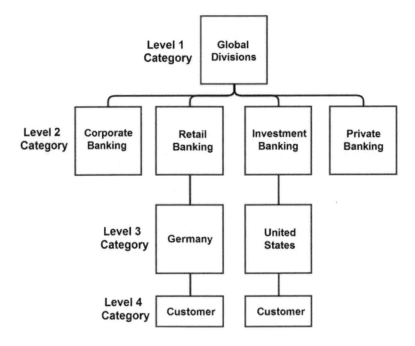

Figure 4.2: Multiple level 4 data categories for customer at a large bank

Summary

- A data category is a logical classification of information to support data governance.

- Data categories are critical to downstream data governance activities, especially data stewardship. If data categories are not established correctly, it will be difficult to identify data stewards.

- Data categories are organized by hierarchy, with level 1 categories containing level 2 categories, level 2 categories containing level 3 categories, and so on.

- Defining data categories requires strong collaboration between data architecture and data governance teams, with an eye to balancing utility with whether a data owner exists organizationally for the proposed category.

- Lower-level categories should reflect the requirements of the organization's various divisions, countries of operation, and legal entities.

5

Data Ownership

Data ownership is the process of identifying individuals who will be accountable for the trustworthiness of data within their purview. As part of BCBS 239 and DFAST compliance, financial institutions need to demonstrate that they have the appropriate controls in place to drive data ownership.

These controls need to be present at multiple levels:

- Does the organization have the appropriate data governance roles (e.g., executive sponsor, data governance executive, data governance lead)?

- Does the organization have the appropriate data stewardship roles to support data ownership (e.g., data executive, managing data steward, data steward)?

- Does the organization have the appropriate groups to act as decision-making bodies (e.g., enterprise data governance council, regional data governance councils, business-specific data governance councils, forums for managing data stewards and data stewards)?

Governance Role: Executive Sponsor

The attesting executive for the BCBS 239 and DFAST reports is generally the executive sponsor for the data governance program. This individual is typically the chief risk officer or the chief financial officer. The executive sponsor holds ultimate accountability for the data governance program. He or she champions data governance with executive staff and holds overall funding for the program.

Governance Role: Data Governance Executive

The data governance executive is accountable for data governance. The data governance executive may also be the chief data officer. Specific responsibilities of the data governance executive include the following:

A. Appoint the data governance lead

B. Approve the data governance framework and roadmap

C. Interact with other members of the executive staff to sell data governance across the enterprise

Governance Role: Data Governance Lead

The data governance lead is accountable for leading data governance on a day-to-day basis. This role will be responsible for the following:

A. Establish an enterprise data governance framework

B. Formulate the data governance roadmap

C. Develop the data governance playbook

D. Lead the enterprise data governance council

E. Collaborate with data architecture to define data categories

F. Identify data owners for data categories

G. Drive the data governance roadmap across metadata and data quality

H. Interact with regulators, compliance, and internal audit to drive the best outcome for the organization in terms of data governance compliance

I. Monitor data governance through dashboards

J. Enforce data governance through periodic data governance audits

Stewardship Role: Data Executive

The data executive is a senior leader who has ultimate responsibility for the trustworthiness of information within a data category. Taking the example from Chapter 4, the data executive for customer data in the U.S. investment bank may be the chief operating officer for the U.S. investment bank. The data executive is responsible for the following:

A. Appoint managing data stewards who have day-to-day oversight responsibility for the data

B. Identify CDEs for a data category

C. Manage business definitions and data quality rules for CDEs

D. Triage and resolve high-impact data quality issues

Stewardship Role: Managing Data Steward

Each data executive will appoint one or more managing data stewards to drive day-to-day activities. The managing data steward may own the same data categories or may own a subset of the data categories as the data executive.

Stewardship Role: Data Steward

Each managing data steward will appoint one or more data stewards to have hands-on responsibility for the data. The responsibilities of the data steward include the following:

A. Define and manage business metadata, including common business vocabularies, allowable values, business rules, and data quality rules

B. Act as subject matter expert in interactions with his or her peers

C. Identify, investigate, and resolve data quality issues

Groups: Enterprise Data Governance Council

The data governance executive needs to establish an overall decision-making body at the enterprise level. The responsibilities of the enterprise data governance council include the following:

A. Set the strategy and roadmap for enterprise data governance

B. Approve the data governance playbook with policies and standards

C. Approve funding for data governance projects including consulting and tools

D. Review progress against data governance milestones

E. Approve the appointment of data executives

F. Manage escalated conflicts, as appropriate

Groups: Region- and Business-Specific Data Governance Councils

Any large, multinational financial services institution may need region- and business-specific data governance councils to address local needs. For example, a multinational financial institution such as the one modeled in Figure 5.1 may have a global data governance council in addition to business-specific councils within corporate banking, retail banking, risk, and treasury. The organization may also need data governance councils in specific countries to address the needs of local regulators.

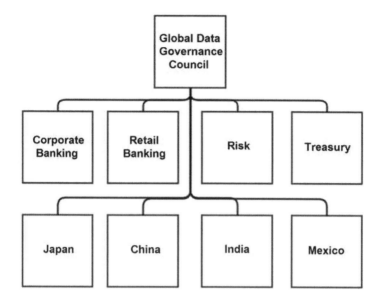

Figure 5.1: A model data governance structure for a global financial institution

Groups: Forums for Managing Data Stewards and Data Stewards

Financial institutions also need forums where managing data stewards and data stewards can resolve issues at their level without bringing matters to the data governance council. Topics to be discussed at these forums include the following:

A. Share information regarding data governance best practices relating to metadata, reference data, and data quality

B. Resolve conflicts before they need to be brought to the data governance council

C. Identify subject matter experts who can resolve data issues

Summary

- Data ownership is the process of identifying individuals who will be accountable for the trustworthiness of data within their purview.

- Data ownership is a key control to support compliance with BCBS 239 and DFAST.

- Data ownership roles break down into data governance roles, data stewardship roles, and decision-making groups.

- Data governance roles include the executive sponsor, the data governance executive, and the data governance lead.

- Data stewardship roles include the data executive, the managing data steward, and the data steward.

- Decision-making groups include the enterprise data governance council, region- and business-specific data governance councils, and forum s for managing data stewards and data stewards.

6

Critical Data Elements

Critical data elements (CDEs) are data elements that are determined to be vital to the success of an organization and represent significant regulatory or operational risk. CDEs may be base attributes (such as Gross Domestic Product) or derived terms (such as Probability of Default). The rule of thumb is that CDEs should generally constitute not more than 5 to 10 percent of the total number of attributes under consideration.

Prioritize Applicable Regulations

Because CDEs have a significant impact on regulatory reporting, the first step is to identify the applicable regulations. As this book is focused on BCBS 239 and DFAST, let's select DFAST for this example.

Select Regulatory Reports

The next step is to select reports that are filed with the regulators. Let's select the annual DFAST 10-50 report that is submitted to the OCC. As discussed earlier, the DFAST 10-50 report collects detailed data on company-run stress tests by national banks and federal savings associations with consolidated assets in the $10 billion to $50 billion range. It should be noted that the OCC DFAST 14A report collects the results of company-run stress tests by banks with more than $50 billion in assets.

Select Key Variables in the Regulatory Reports

The next step is to select key variables in the regulatory reports. Taking the DFAST 10-50 report example further, the company-run stress test is based on a number of scenario variables across geographic regions.[1] Using the example discussed in Chapter 4, where the Level 1 data category is **Risk** and the Level 2 data category is **Scenario Variables**, Table 6.1 shows the 28 example variables classified as CDEs.

Table 6.1: Scenario Variables Classified as Critical Data Elements		
Level 3 Category	**Level 4 Category**	**Critical Data Elements**
United States	Economic development variables	1. Real GDP growth 2. Nominal GDP growth 3. Real disposable income growth 4. Nominal disposable income growth 5. Unemployment rate 6. Consumer Price Index inflation rate
	Aggregate measures of asset prices or financial conditions	7. House price index 8. Commercial real estate price index 9. Dow Jones Total Stock Market Index 10. Market Volatility Index (VIX)
	Interest rates	11. 3-month Treasury bill rate 12. Yield on the 5-year Treasury bond 13. Yield on the 10-year Treasury bond 14. Yield on a 10-year BBB corporate security 15. Interest rate associated with a conforming, conventional, fixed-rate, 30-year mortgage 16. Prime rate
Euro area	Not applicable	17. Euro area real GDP growth 18. Euro area inflation 19. Euro area bilateral dollar exchange rate ($/euro)

---

[1] Board of Governors of the Federal Reserve System, Dodd-Frank Act Stress Test 2014: Supervisory Stress Test Methodology and Results, http://www.federalreserve.gov/bankinforeg/stress-tests/2014-appendix-a.htm

Developing Asia	Not applicable	20. Developing Asia real GDP growth 21. Developing Asia inflation 22. Developing Asia bilateral dollar exchange rate (F/USD, index, base=2000 Q1)
Japan	Not applicable	23. Japan real GDP growth 24. Japan inflation 25. Japan bilateral dollar exchange rate (yen/USD)
United Kingdom	Not applicable	26. U.K. real GDP growth 27. U.K. inflation 28. U.K. bilateral dollar exchange rate (USD/pound)

Define Template for Critical Data Elements

Business Glossary

Basel Committee on Banking Supervision, Principles for Effective Risk Data Aggregation and Risk Reporting, *January 2013, Principle 3 – Accuracy and Integrity, Paragraph 37*

As a precondition, a bank should have a "dictionary" of the concepts used, such that data is defined consistently across an organization.

In order to capture metadata relating to CDEs, the data governance team needs to provide data stewards with a template such as the one shown in Table 6.2.

Table 6.2: Template for Critical Data Elements	
Attribute	**Description**
Name	Name of business term that is classified as CDE
Level 1 data category	Name of level 1 data category in the information hierarchy (e.g., Risk)
Level 2 data category	Name of level 2 data category in the information hierarchy, if applicable
Level 3 data category	Name of level 3 data category in the information hierarchy, if applicable
Level 4 data category	Name of level 4 data category in the information hierarchy, if applicable
Definition	Meaning of the business term within the business context
Definition source	Source that provides the definition for the business term, such as the OCC

Acronym	Shorthand formed from initial letters of term (e.g., LGD for Loss Given Default, EAD for Exposure at Default)
Calculation	Algorithm used to produce a business term
Authoritative data source	Approved repository for a given business term, data element, or attribute
Synonyms	Relation between business terms with the same definition (e.g., vendor and supplier)
Is a type of/ Has types	Relation to show that a business term is a type of another (e.g., Seasonal GDP, Real GDP, and Nominal GDP are types of GDP; similarly, GDP has types Seasonal GDP, Real GDP, and Nominal GDP)
Related terms	Relation to link business terms that are not synonyms or types (e.g., Real GDP and Real GDP growth are related terms)
Reference data	Defined set of values for a business term (e.g., U.S. state codes)
Data consumers	Business terms, reports, models, and other artifacts that consume the CDE
Data producers	Business terms, models, columns, fields, and other artifacts that produce the CDE
Data quality rules	Rules to define data quality classified by data quality dimension
Data executive	Name of individual who is ultimately accountable for the data
Data executive title	Title of individual who is ultimately accountable for the data
Managing data steward	Name of individual who has oversight responsibility for the data
Managing data steward title	Title of individual who has oversight responsibility for the data
Data steward	Name of individual who works with data on a day-to-day basis
Data steward title	Title of individual who works with data on a day-to-day basis

Populate Template for Critical Data Elements

Once the templates are provided, the data stewards need to populate the template for each CDE. Table 6.3 shows a sample populated template, using the "Developing Asia Inflation" CDE.

Table 6.3: CDE Template for Developing Asia Inflation	
Attribute	**Description**
Name	Developing Asia Inflation
Level 1 data category	Risk
Level 2 data category	Scenario variables
Level 3 data category	Developing Asia
Level 4 data category	Not applicable
Definition	Staff calculations based on Chinese National Bureau of Statistics via CEIC; Indian Ministry of Statistics and Programme Implementation via Haver; Labour Bureau of India via CEIC; National Statistical Office of Korea via CEIC; Census and Statistic Department of Hong Kong via CEIC; and Taiwan Directorate-General of Budget, Accounting, and Statistics via CEIC[2]
Authoritative data source	CEIC
Reports that consume this data	OCC DFAST 10-50
Business terms that consume this information	Not applicable
Business terms that are consumed by this information	Developing Asia
Related terms	Consumer Price Index inflation rate, euro area inflation, Japan inflation, U.K. inflation
Data executive	Jane Wells
Data executive title	Vice President, Risk
Managing data steward	Jane Doe
Managing data steward title	Manager, Risk
Data steward	Jack Smith
Data steward title	Risk Data Manager

---

[2] Board of Governors of the Federal Reserve System, Dodd-Frank Act Stress Test 2014: Supervisory Stress Test Methodology and Results, http://www.federalreserve.gov/bankinforeg/stress-tests/2014-appendix-a.htm

Derive Additional Critical Data Elements That Are Consumed Upstream

Data stewards should identify additional business terms that are consumed by the CDEs that have already been identified. Taking the example in Table 6.3 further, Developing Asia is also a CDE because it is used as an input into Developing Asia Inflation. The definition for Developing Asia is "the nominal GDP-weighted aggregate of China, India, South Korea, Hong Kong SAR, and Taiwan."[3]

Link Critical Data Elements That May Have Different Meanings in Different Contexts

Some business terms may have different meanings in different contexts. For example, Figure 6.1 represents probability of default as a CDE, which is part of the exposure category. However, because there are multiple types of probability of default, including Point-in-Time, Through-the-Cycle, Stressed PD, and Unstressed PD, these terms must also be treated as CDEs.

The definitions and other business metadata relating to the different types of Probability of Default are shown below:

Term: Probability of Default
Data category: Exposure
Acronym: PD
Definition: Financial term describing the likelihood of a default over a particular time horizon. It provides an estimate of the likelihood that a borrower will be unable to meet its debt obligations.[4]
Types: Point-in-Time, Through-the-Cycle, Stressed PD, Unstressed PD

---

[3] Office of the Comptroller of the Currency, U.S. Department of the Treasury, *Annual Stress Test Baseline, Adverse, and Severely Adverse Scenarios*, January 28, 2016.

[4] https://en.wikipedia.org/wiki/Probability_of_default

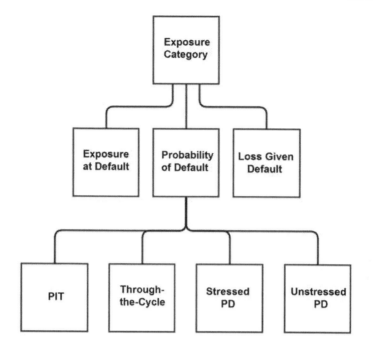

Figure 6.1: Linking various types of probability of Default to consider them as CDEs

Term: Point-in-Time
Data category: Exposure
Acronym: PIT
Definition: Likelihood that measures default risk based on an assessment of the borrower's current condition and/or most likely future condition over the course of the chosen time horizon. As such, the internal rating changes as the borrower's condition changes over the course of the credit/business cycle.[5]
Is a type of: Probability of Default
Related terms: Through-the-Cycle, Stressed PD, Unstressed PD

---

[5] Basel Committee on Banking Supervision, *The Internal Ratings-Based Approach*, January 2001, http://www.bis.org/publ/bcbsca05.pdf

Term: Through-the-Cycle
Data category: Exposure
Acronym: TTC
Definition: Likelihood that measures default risk based on an assessment of the borrower's riskiness in a worst-case, "bottom of the cycle" scenario (i.e., its condition under stress). In this case, a borrower's rating would tend to stay the same over the course of the credit/business cycle.[6]
Is a type of: Probability of Default
Related terms: Point-in-Time, Stressed PD, Unstressed PD

Term: Stressed PD
Data category: Exposure
Definition: Financial term describing the likelihood of a default during stress/crisis situations. It provides an estimate of the likelihood that a borrower will be unable to meet its debt obligations during stress/crisis situations.[7]
Is a type of: Probability of Default
Related terms: Point-in-Time, Through-the-Cycle, Unstressed PD

Term: Unstressed PD
Data category: Exposure
Definition: Estimate that the obligor will default over a particular time horizon considering the current macroeconomic as well as obligor-specific information. This implies that if the macroeconomic conditions deteriorate, the PD of an obligor will tend to increase while it will tend to decrease if economic conditions improve.[8]
Is a type of: Probability of Default
Related terms: Point-in-Time, Through-the-Cycle, Stressed PD

---

[6] Basel Committee on Banking Supervision, *The Internal Ratings-Base Approach*, January 2001, http://www.bis.org/publ/bcbsca05.pdf

[7] https://en.wikipedia.org/wiki/Probability_of_default#Stressed_and_Unstressed_PD

[8] https://en.wikipedia.org/wiki/Probability_of_default#Stressed_and_Unstressed_PD

Summary

- Critical data elements (CDEs) are the 5 to 10 percent of data elements that are determined to be vital to the success of an organization and represent significant regulatory or operational risk.

- CDEs may be base attributes (such as Gross Domestic Product) or derived terms (such as Probability of Default).

- CDEs should be driven by key fields in regulatory reports, as they identify where data needs to be most complete in order to manage risks effectively.

- Data governance teams should establish a template to gather metadata for CDEs.

7

Data Quality

Data quality management is a discipline that includes methods to measure and improve the quality and integrity of an organization's data. Data quality management is absolutely foundational to compliance with BCBS 239 and DFAST data governance.

Agree on the Data Quality Dimensions for the Data Governance Program

According to DAMA UK in *The Six Primary Dimensions for Data Quality Assessment* (October 2013), data quality dimension is a recognized term used by data management professionals to describe a characteristic, attribute, or facet of data that can be measured or assessed against defined standards in order to determine the quality of data. Although there are no industry-standard definitions for data quality dimensions, Table 7.1 lists some data quality dimensions and the way they can be used to create data quality rules.

Table 7.1: Data Quality Dimensions

Data Quality Dimension	Definition	Sample Data Quality Rules
1. Completeness	The degree to which data elements are populated	General Ledger Account ID cannot be NULL
2. Conformity	The degree to which data elements correspond to expected formats or valid values or ranges of values	State should be from the agreed-upon list of code values for state
3. Consistency	The degree of relational integrity between data elements and other data elements	The insurance policy expiration date should be greater than or equal to the policy effective date
4. Synchronization	The degree to which data elements are consistent from one data store to the next	Customer ID in the master data hub must be the same as the one in the legacy customer file
5. Uniqueness	The degree to which data elements are unique within a data store	Customer IDs should be unique in the customer reference table
6. Timeliness	The degree to which data is available on a timely basis	Global value at risk must be calculated by 10 a.m. Eastern time Monday to Friday
7. Accuracy	The degree to which data elements are accurate	Customer NAICS code must be accurate

Define Template for Data Quality Rules

Data Validation Rules

Basel Committee on Banking Supervision, Principles for Effective Risk Data Aggregation and Risk Reporting, *January 2013, Principle 7 – Accuracy, Paragraph 53(b)*

To ensure the accuracy of the reports, a bank should maintain, at a minimum…automated and manual edit and reasonableness checks, including an inventory of the validation rules that are applied to quantitative information. The inventory should include explanations of the conventions used to describe any mathematical or logical relationships that should be verified through these validations or checks.

The data governance team needs to provide data stewards with a template to capture data quality rules. Table 7.2 shows an example of such a template.

Table 7.2: Template for Data Quality Rules	
Attribute	**Description**
Name	Name of data quality rule
Level 1 data category	Name of level 1 data category in the information hierarchy (e.g., Risk)
Level 2 data category	Name of level 2 data category in the information hierarchy, if applicable
Level 3 data category	Name of level 3 data category in the information hierarchy, if applicable
Level 4 data category	Name of level 4 data category in the information hierarchy, if applicable
Description	Description of the data quality rule in a business context
Dimension	Data quality dimension relating to the rule
Calculation	Algorithm used to produce the data quality rule
Critical data elements	Mapping to CDEs that are governed by the data quality rule
Technical field names	Mapping to columns, fields, tables, schemas, and databases that contain the source data for the data quality rule
Technical data quality expression	Mapping to physical data quality expressions, such as SQL scripts that operationalize the data quality rule by source system
Data executive	Name of individual who is ultimately accountable for the data quality rule
Data executive title	Title of individual who is ultimately accountable for the data quality rule
Managing data steward	Name of individual who has oversight responsibility for the data quality rule
Managing data steward title	Title of individual who has oversight responsibility for the data quality rule
Data steward	Name of individual who works with the data quality rule on a day-to-day basis
Data steward title	Title of individual who works with the data quality rule on a day-to-day basis

Develop Data Quality Rules

The data governance team should document data quality rules in the business glossary (see Table 7.3).

Table 7.3: Sample Data Quality Rules		
Dimension	**CDE**	**Data Quality Rule**
Consistency	Credit Type (type of exposure including secured and unsecured)	If loan is secured, then the value of collateral should be greater than null.
Consistency	Credit Type	If loan is unsecured, then the value of collateral should be null.
Completeness	GL Account Identifier	GL Account ID cannot be null.
Consistency	Customer ID	All Obligor IDs in the exposure tables must exist in the customer reference table.
Conformity	Default Flag	Default Flag must always be "Y" or "N" and cannot be null or blank.
Consistency	Probability of Default	If PD is 1, then loan loss provision should be 100 percent of loan outstanding balance.
Synchronization	Exposure at Default	For a given customer ID, exposure at default in the data warehouse and credit risk model should be the same.
Conformity	LGD Rating Code	Loss Given Default (LGD) Rating Code should be between 1 and 12.
Consistency	Instrument Effective Date	Instrument Effective Date can never be null or earlier than "01-01-1996" or later than the last day of the previous month.
Consistency	CUSIP Number	All CUSIP numbers should be present as "Security IDs" in the securities master. Committee on Uniform Securities Identification Procedures (CUSIP) Number identifies most financial instruments, including stocks of all registered U.S. and Canadian companies, commercial paper, and U.S. government and municipal bonds.
Timeliness	VaR	Global Value at Risk (VaR) must be calculated by 10 a.m. Eastern time Monday to Friday.

Accuracy	NAICS Code	Customer NAICS Code must be accurate. Because accuracy of Customer NAICS Codes is difficult to measure in practice, a monthly test check of at least 80 customer records will be used as a proxy to determine the accuracy of customer NAICS codes.
		The actual calculation of NAICS code accuracy is as follows:
		Number of accurate customer NAICS Codes in the month / Number of files reviewed in the month = Accuracy percentage of customer NAICS codes in the month

Create a Data Quality Scorecard

A data quality scorecard is a useful tool to report on the results of a data quality program. The data quality scorecard should be shared with key stakeholders, including the data governance council, data executives, managing data stewards, and data stewards. Table 7.4 shows a sample data quality scorecard for the home data category at a bank. The scorecard consists of three data quality rules, which have been weighted equally. In practice, a typical data quality scorecard may consist of hundreds, if not thousands, of rules.

Table 7.4: Data Quality Scorecard for Home Data Category			
Data Quality Rule	**Dimension**	**Weight**	**Home**
Appraised value of home cannot be null	Completeness	33%	95%
Appraisal data cannot be more than six months prior to the effective date of the loan	Consistency	33%	90%
Borrower ID must be consistent with the customer ID in the master data hub	Synchronization	33%	85%
Overall Score			**90%**

Table 7.5 shows the data quality scorecard for the retail banking division of the same bank. The scorecard rolls up the dashboards for the home data category seen in Table 7.4 and the auto data category. Each data category has been assigned a relative weight based on their respective impact on risk-weighted assets.

Table 7.5: Data Quality Scorecard for Retail Banking Division			
Description	Retail Bank	Home	Auto
Weight	100%	75%	25%
Data Quality Score	87.5%	90%	80%

Finally, Table 7.6 shows the data quality scorecard for the enterprise. This scorecard rolls up the dashboards for the retail and commercial bank. Each division has been assigned a relative weight based on their respective impact on risk-weighted assets.

Table 7.6: Data Quality Scorecard for the Enterprise			
Description	Enterprise	Retail Bank	Commercial Bank
Weight	100%	60%	40%
Data Quality Score	84.5%	87.5%	80%

Define Criteria to Triage Data Quality Issues

Data Quality Exceptions

Basel Committee on Banking Supervision, Principles for Effective Risk Data Aggregation and Risk Reporting, *January 2013, Principle 7 – Accuracy, Paragraph 53(c)*

To ensure the accuracy of the reports, a bank should maintain, at a minimum...integrated procedures for identifying, reporting and explaining data errors or weaknesses in data integrity via exceptions reports.

Data quality processes will typically generate hundreds, if not thousands, of exceptions. Data stewards lack the capacity to address every data quality exception. Data executives should define criteria to triage data quality issues so that data stewards focus on only the high impact exceptions. Triage criteria should include the impact on risk-weighted assets, revenues, and profitability. The data governance team should create a template to triage data quality issues, such as the sample in Table 7.7.

Table 7.7: Template to Triage Data Quality Issues	
Attribute	**Description**
Issue ID	The unique identifier for the data quality issue
Date issue identified	Date when the data quality issue was identified
Short description	One-sentence description of the data quality issue
Long description	Lengthy description of the data quality issue
Source system	Name of the source system where the data quality check was performed
Schema	Name of the schema in the source system where the data quality check was performed
Table	Name of the table in the source system where the data quality check was performed
Column	Name of the column in the source system where the data quality check was performed
Initial priority	Priority assigned by the data steward on an interim basis
Data quality rule	Name of the data quality rule linked to the CDE (e.g., the "Customer ID should not be null" data quality rule is linked to the "Customer ID" CDE)
Data quality dimension	Name of the data quality dimension for the data quality rule (e.g., completeness)
Number of records	Number of records where the data quality check was performed
Number of issues	Number of records where data quality issues were discovered
Financial impact	Dollar impact of the data quality issue on revenues, costs, or risk-weighted assets, if known (qualitative statements are acceptable if the impact is not quantifiable)
Final priority	High, medium, or low priority assigned by the data steward in consultation with the managing data steward
Individual who discovered the issue	Name of individual who discovered the data quality issue
Title of individual who discovered the issue	Title of individual who discovered the data quality issue

Remediate Data Quality Issues

Once data quality issues have been prioritized, they need to be assigned to owners. The data governance team should use a template, such as the sample shown in Table 7.8, to track the resolution of data quality issues.

Table 7.8: Template to Track Data Quality Issue Resolution	
Attribute	**Description**
Short description	One-sentence description of the data quality issue
Long description	Lengthy description of the data quality issue
Final priority	High, medium, or low priority assigned by the data steward in consultation with the managing data steward
Source system	Name of the source system where the data quality check was performed
Issue ID	The unique identifier for the data quality issue in the issuer tracker
Data issue identified	Date when the data quality issue was identified
Remediation activity	A brief description of the activities to resolve the data quality issue
Assigned individual	Name of individual who has been assigned responsibility to resolve the issue
Title of assigned individual	Title of individual who has been assigned responsibility to resolve the issue
Target completion date	Target date for resolution of the data quality issue
Status	Status of the data quality issue (e.g., closed, in-progress, deferred)
Remediation closure date	Actual close date of the data quality issue

Summary

- The identification, reporting, triage, and resolution of data quality issues are critical to compliance with BCBS 239 and DFAST.

- The first step is to standardize the data quality dimensions: completeness, conformity, consistency, synchronization, uniqueness, timeliness, and accuracy.

- Data stewards should document data quality rules in the business glossary for each CDE. These data quality rules should be classified by data quality dimension.

- A data quality scorecard should report on the overall state of data quality.

- A triage template should support the prioritization of data quality issues based on the impact on risk-weighted assets, revenues, and profitability.

- Data stewards should remediate prioritized data quality issues using a resolution template.

8

Analytical Models and End User Computing

Model Governance

Basel Committee on Banking Supervision, Principles for Effective Risk Data Aggregation and Risk Reporting, *January 2013, Scope and initial considerations, Paragraph 17*

These Principles also apply to all key internal risk management models, including but not limited to, Pillar 1 regulatory capital models (e.g., internal ratings-based approaches for credit risk and advanced measurement approaches for operational risk), Pillar 2 capital models and other key risk management models (e.g., value-at-risk).

Manage Model Metadata

Model Inventory

DFAST Reporting Instructions, OCC Reporting Form DFAST-14A, March 2016

Banks must provide a comprehensive inventory of models used in the projection of losses, revenues, expenses, balances, risk-weighted assets, and the status of validation/independent review for each. The inventory or list of models should be organized around the DFAST-14A line items. The documentation should clearly map each model/methodology listed in the inventory to a specific product or line item in the DFAST-14A schedules. In addition, each model description should include details of any model overlays or driver-based tools and should quantify how the model outcome changes when the overlay/driver-based tool is applied.

The inventory should identify, at a minimum, the name of the model, model owner, model output and intended use (i.e., model purpose), and dates of completed or planned validation activities.

In order to document and inventory their models, the model governance team needs to capture metadata regarding models that are used for DFAST and BCBS 239 using a template such as the sample shown in Table 8.1.

Table 8.1: Template for Model Metadata	
Attribute	**Description**
Model ID	Unique identifier for the model
Name	Name of the model
Description	Description of the model
Business purpose	Business use of the model
Methodology	Methodology used to develop the model (e.g., regression analysis, rules, logistic regression, random forest)
Application	Application used to develop the model (e.g., SAS®, R, Hadoop)
Level 1 model category	Name of the Level 1 category where the model can be best classified (e.g., credit risk models, market risk models, liquidity risk models, operational risk models)
Level 2 model category	Name of the Level 2 category where the model can be best classified, if applicable
Report and line item	Name of the line item in the report to which the model applies (e.g., DFAST-14A Income Statement – Line Item 29 – Losses on Credit Cards)
Input variables	Names of the variables used as inputs into the models (e.g., GDP)
Input models	IDs of models that are used as input into this model
Business rules governing inputs	Business rules that govern variable and model inputs into this model (e.g., only use seasonal GDP as an input into the model)
Output variables	Names of the variables that are outputs from this model
Dependent models	IDs of models that depend on the outputs of this model
Business rules governing outputs	Business rules that govern the outputs of this model
Model creator	Name of individual who created the model
Model creator department	Department of individual who created the model
Model owner	Name of individual who owns the model
Model owner department	Department of individual who owns the model

Model create date	Date that the model was created
Model deployment date	Date that the model was deployed
Model validation date	Date that the model was independently validated or will be validated
Model validation owner	Name of the individual who independently validated or will validate the model
Model validation department	Department of the individual who independently validated or will validate the model

Conduct Independent Model Validation

According to the Basel guidelines for Model Validation of Expected Credit Losses (ECL)[1], a bank should have policies and procedures in place to appropriately validate models used to assess and measure expected credit losses.

ECL assessment and measurement may involve models and assumption-based estimates for risk identification and measurement. Models may be used in various aspects of the ECL assessment and measurement process at both the individual transaction and overall portfolio levels, including credit grading, credit risk identification, measurement of ECL allowances for accounting purposes, stress testing, and capital allocation. ECL assessment and measurement models should consider the impact of changes to borrower and credit risk-related variables such as changes in probability of defaults (PDs), loss given defaults (LGDs), exposure amounts, collateral values, migration of default probabilities, and internal borrower credit risk grades based on historical, current, and reasonable and supportable forward-looking information, including macroeconomic factors.

Because the development and use of ECL assessment and measurement models involves extensive judgment, effective model validation policies and procedures are crucial. A bank should have robust policies and procedures in place to validate the accuracy and consistency of its model-based rating systems and processes and the estimation of all relevant risk components, at the outset of model usage and on an ongoing basis. Model validation should be conducted when the ECL models are

---

[1] Basel Committee on Banking Supervision, *Guidance on Credit Risk and Accounting for Expected Credit Losses*, December 2015, Principle 5, ECL Model Validation, http://www.bis.org/bcbs/publ/d350.pdf

initially developed and when significant changes are made to the models. A bank should regularly (for example, annually) review its ECL models.

A sound model validation framework should include, but not be limited to, the following elements:

- *Clear roles and responsibilities for model validation with adequate independence and competence*

  Model validation should be performed independently of the model development process and by staff with the necessary experience and expertise. Model validation involves ensuring that the models are suitable for their proposed usage, at the outset and on an ongoing basis. The findings and outcomes of model validation should be reported in a prompt and timely manner to the appropriate level of authority.

- *An appropriate model validation scope and methodology including a systematic process of evaluating the model's robustness, consistency, and accuracy as well as its continued relevance to the underlying portfolio*

  An effective model validation process should also enable potential limitations of a model to be identified and addressed on a timely basis. The scope for validation should include a review of model inputs, model design, and model outputs/performance.

  o *Model inputs*—The bank should have internally established quality and reliability standards on data (historical, current, and forward-looking information) used as model inputs. Data used to estimate ECL allowances should be relevant to the bank's portfolios and as far as possible accurate, reliable, and complete (i.e., without exclusions that could bias ECL estimates). Validation should ensure that the data used meet these standards.

  o *Model design*—For model design, validation should demonstrate that the underlying theory of the model is conceptually sound, recognized, and generally accepted for its intended purpose. From a forward-looking perspective, validation should also assess the extent to which the model, at the overall model and individual risk factor level, can take into consideration changes in the economic or credit environment, as well as changes to portfolio business profile or strategy, without significantly reducing model robustness.

o *Model output/performance*—The bank should have internally established standards for acceptable model performance. Where performance thresholds are significantly breached, remedial actions to the extent of model recalibration or redevelopment should be considered.

• *Comprehensive documentation of the model validation framework and process*

This includes documenting the validation procedures performed, any changes in validation methodology and tools, the range of data used, validation results, and any remedial actions taken where necessary. Banks should ensure that the documentation is regularly reviewed and updated.

• *A review of the model validation process by independent parties (e.g., internal or external parties) to evaluate the overall effectiveness of the model validation process and the independence of the model validation process from the development process*

The findings of the review should be reported in a prompt and timely manner to the appropriate level of authority (e.g., senior management, audit committee).

Establish End User Computing Governance Policies

End User Computing Governance

Basel Committee on Banking Supervision, Principles for Effective Risk Data Aggregation and Risk Reporting, *January 2013, Principle 3 – Accuracy and Integrity, Paragraph 36(b)*

A bank should aggregate risk data in a way that is accurate and reliable. Where a bank relies on manual processes and desktop applications (e.g., spreadsheets, databases) and has specific risk units that use these applications for software development, it should have effective mitigants in place (e.g., end-user computing policies and procedures) and other effective controls that are consistently applied across the bank's processes.

DFAST Reporting Instructions, OCC Reporting Form DFAST-14A, March 2016

The model inventory also should include significant end-user computing applications that support projections of losses, revenues, expenses, balances, and risk-weighted assets. EUCs include spreadsheets, databases, and desktop applications (e.g., queries/scripts).

An end user computing (EUC) application is a solution created to meet a specific business, financial, risk management, or operational requirement and is outside the purview of the IT department. EUCs are generally not supported by IT and do not have an application owner. Banks typically generate a significant volume of end user computing applications in the form of spreadsheets, databases, and SAS files, which may be stored on desktops or in SharePoint repositories.

Banks need to establish policies with respect to EUC governance:

- *Scope*—Define the scope of the EUC governance program. DFAST reporting guidelines require banks to maintain an inventory of significant EUCs. A potential approach would be to only cover EUCs that have a material impact on losses, revenues, expenses, balances, and risk-weighted assets.

- *Ownership*—EUCs owners should be identified. The responsibilities of an EUC owner should also be clearly defined. For example, an EUC owner should be accountable to capture the appropriate metadata and revalidate the EUC metadata on a periodic basis.

- *Metadata management*—EUCs should be integrated into the metadata management process. The model metadata template also applies to EUC metadata. The EUC governance team should review the quality of EUC metadata on a periodic basis for completeness and accuracy.

- *Security and privacy*—EUC governance policies should also ensure that any personally identifiable information or other sensitive data is protected. This is an area of concern from an operational risk perspective.

- *Revalidation*—Critical EUC models should be subject to a periodic validation process, similar to the model validation process.

Integrate Models and End User Computing into Data Lineage

Data governance teams should integrate models and EUCs into the end-to-end data lineage. We will discuss more about data lineage in the next chapter.

Summary

- BCBS 239 and DFAST compliance principles are also applicable to internal risk management models.

- Model metadata should be captured using a template to support compliance efforts.

- Robust policies and procedures for model validation are crucial to verify that the results produced by models are accurate and consistent. Model validation should be conducted when models are initially developed, after significant changes, and on a regular basis.

- Sound model validation should include clear roles and responsibilities independent of the development process; a systematic evaluation of the robustness, consistency, and accuracy of the model as well each model's ongoing relevance to the underlying portfolio; a comprehensive documentation of the model validation framework and process; and a review of the model validation process by internal or external independent parties.

- Prompt and timely reporting of any issues is vital to all steps of the model validation process.

- EUC applications are solutions created to meet a specific business, financial, risk management, or operational requirement and commonly do not have an IT owner.

- EUC applications should be a component of the model inventory under BCBS 239 and DFAST compliance regimes and require specific governance policies.

- Both risk models and EUCs should be integrated into end-to-end data lineage.

9

Data Lineage

Data lineage provides an audit trail from source to target. Data lineage pertains to either business or technical lineage and is an important component of compliance with BCBS 239 and DFAST.

Business Lineage

The data governance team should be able to demonstrate lineage back to source data from a business perspective. For example, in the case shown in Figure 9.1, business users should be able to demonstrate the lineage of global value at risk (VaR) back to source artifacts, including CDEs and data quality rules.

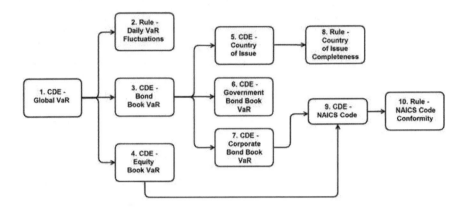

Figure 9.1: The business lineage for global VaR

Table 9.1 discusses each component of the business lineage for the global VaR application.

Table 9.1: Business Lineage for Global VaR		
Artifact	**Artifact Type**	**Description**
1. Global VaR	CDE	Business term associated with the calculation of global VaR on a daily basis.
2. Daily VaR fluctuations	Data quality rule	Data quality rule that governs global VaR based on the accuracy dimension. The rule states that global VaR should not fluctuate by more than 8 percent on a daily basis in the absence of abnormal market conditions.
3. Bond book VaR	CDE	Business term associated with the calculation of VaR for the bond book. This business term is an input into the calculation of global VaR.
4. Equity book VaR	CDE	Business term associated with the calculation of VaR for the equity book. This business term is an input into the calculation of global VaR.
5. Country of issue	CDE	Business term associated with the country of issue for bonds. Because country of issue has a significant impact on default risk, it also drives the calculation of bond book VaR.
6. Government bond book VaR	CDE	Business term associated with the calculation of VaR for the government bond book. This business term is an input into the calculation of bond book VaR.

7. Corporate bond book VaR	CDE	Business term associated with the calculation of VaR for the corporate bond book. This business term is an input into the calculation of bond book VaR.
8. Country of issue	Data quality rule	Data quality rule that governs country of issue based on the completeness dimension. The rule states that bond country of issue should not be null or blank.
9. NAICS code	CDE	Business term that denotes a code set used by the U.S. government to classify businesses for statistical purposes. NAICS code provides an input into the industry-specific default risk for the corporate bond and equity books.
10. NAICS code conformity	Data quality rule	Data quality rule that states that NAICS code for a corporate bond or equity must conform to the list of reference codes.

Technical Lineage

Business lineage covers the traceability of business artifacts from source to target. However, regulators also require banks to answer questions such as these:

- Where did this data come from?
- Where is it going?
- What happens to it along the way?

This necessitates providing technical lineage, such as that shown in Figure 9.2, which includes systems, transformations, and other technical information in addition to the artifacts provided in the business lineage.

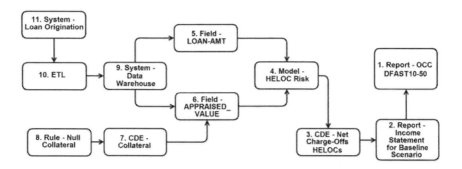

Figure 9.2: Technical lineage for OCC DFAST 10-50 report

Table 9.2 discusses each component of the technical lineage for the OCC DFAST 10-50 report.

Table 9.2: Technical Lineage for OCC DFAST 10-50 Report		
Artifact	**Artifact Type**	**Description**
1. OCC DFAST 10-50	Report	Report submitted to the OCC by banks with assets from $10 billion to $50 billion.
2. Income statement for baseline scenario	Report	Worksheet in report that shows income statement for the baseline scenario.
3. Net charge-offs HELOCs	CDE	Business term relating to write-downs associated with home equity lines of credit.
4. HELOC risk model	Risk model	Risk model associated with HELOC charge-offs for the baseline scenario.
5. LOAN_AMT	Field	Input variable for the HELOC risk model pertaining to the loan amount.
6. APPRAISED_ VALUE	Field	Input variable for the HELOC risk model pertaining to the appraised value for the home.
7. Collateral	CDE	Business term associated with the collateral offered for a loan.
8. Null collateral	Data quality rule	Data quality rule that governs collateral based on the conformity dimension. The rule states that the value of collateral for secured loans cannot be null or blank. In other words, the APPRAISED_ VALUE field for HELOCs cannot be null or blank.
9. Data warehouse	System	LOAN_AMT and APPRAISED_ VALUE fields are sourced from the data warehouse.
10. ETL	Data transformation	ETL job that transforms data from the loan origination system into the data warehouse.
11. Loan origination	System	Loan origination system that is the source system for HELOC data.

Authoritative Data Source

> **Authoritative Source for Risk Data**
>
> *Basel Committee on Banking Supervision,* Principles for Effective Risk Data Aggregation and Risk Reporting, *January 2013, Principle 3 – Accuracy and Integrity, Paragraph 36(d)*
>
> A bank should strive towards a single authoritative source for risk data per each type of risk.

An authoritative data source is a trusted source of data, which has been sanctioned as a source for general reuse by data architecture and data governance. Each data category should be tied out to the authoritative data source within the metadata repository.

Summary

- The data governance team should be able to demonstrate the lineage of data from key regulatory reports back to the source.

- Business lineage provides traceability from a business perspective, including reports, models, CDEs, and data quality rules.

- Technical lineage provides traceability that includes systems, transformations, and other technical information in addition to the artifacts provided in the business lineage.

- Data lineage should include traceability to an authoritative data source.

10

Data Service Level Agreements

> **Data Service Level Agreements**
>
> *Basel Committee on Banking Supervision,* Principles for Effective Risk Data Aggregation and Risk Reporting, *January 2013, Principle 1 – Governance, Paragraph 27*
>
> A bank's board and senior management should promote the identification, assessment and management of data quality risks as part of its overall risk management framework. The framework should include agreed service level standards for both outsourced and in-house risk data-related processes, and a firm's policies on data confidentiality, integrity and availability, as well as risk management policies.
>
> *Basel Committee on Banking Supervision,* Principles for Effective Risk Data Aggregation and Risk Reporting, *January 2013, Principle 5 – Timeliness, Paragraph 44*
>
> A bank's risk data aggregation capabilities should ensure that it is able to produce aggregate risk information on a timely basis to meet all risk management reporting requirements.

Data Service Level Agreements (SLAs) are contracts that govern the quality, timeliness, security, and privacy of data as it moves across the enterprise between consumers and producers. Data SLAs are critical to establish a common set of standards between producers and consumers.

Establish Template for Data SLAs

The data governance team should use a template, such as the example shown in Table 10.1, for data SLAs.

Table 10.1: Template for Data SLAs	
Attribute	**Description**
Name	One-sentence description of the data SLA
Business capability	Description of the business capability that is enabled by the data movement (e.g., timely submission of European VaR to support daily calculation of Global VaR)
Producing executive	Name of the executive who owns the producing application
Title of producing executive	Title of the executive who owns the producing application (e.g., VP, Market Risk – Europe)
Consuming executive	Name of the executive who owns the consuming application
Title of consuming executive	Title of the executive who owns the consuming application (e.g., VP, Global Market Risk)
Dates	Effective date and renewal date of the data SLA
Data feeds	Details about database, schemas, tables, columns, and views regarding data being shared
Preceding batch jobs and data loads	Name, frequency, required completion time, and dependencies of preceding batch jobs and data loads
Downstream batch jobs and data loads	Name, frequency, required completion time, and dependencies of downstream batch jobs and data loads
Data quality thresholds	Acceptable thresholds for data quality by CDE and data quality dimension
Approach to data quality checks	Description of approach to data quality checks (e.g., manual vs. automated, frequency, name of data quality tool, owner)
Source data	Name of database, schema, tables, and columns for data quality checks
Data quality dashboard	Description of approach to data quality dashboards (e.g., manual vs. automated, frequency, name of data quality tool, owner, format for delivery to consumers including by email)
Remediation process	Description of remediation process if acceptable thresholds of data quality are not met
Late delivery escalation procedures	Description of procedures if data is not delivered within the agreed-upon window (e.g., email notification)

Chain Multiple Data SLAs
to Create Interlocking Contracts

Data SLAs can be chained together to drive interlocking contracts across the organization. For example, in Figure 10.1, the global VaR team has established data SLAs with their European, U.S., and Asia-Pacific counterparts to support the calculation of global VaR on a daily basis. Similarly, the European VaR team has established data SLAs with the Eurozone, U.K., and Swiss VaR teams. Finally, the Asia-Pacific VaR team has established similar contracts with the Japan and China VaR teams. These data SLAs are critical because global VaR may be calculated incorrectly if a feed is delayed or has bad data.

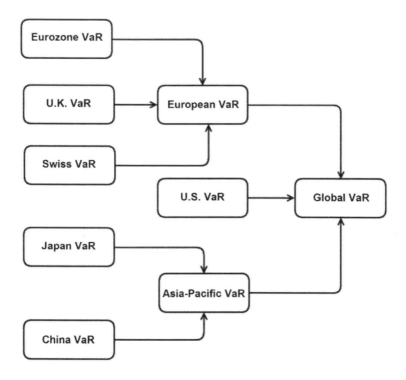

Figure 10.1: Data SLAs that have been chained together to support the daily calculation of global VaR

Summary

- Data SLAs are critical contracts that govern the quality, timeliness, security, and privacy of data as it moves across the enterprise.

- Data SLAs should be an important component of BCBS 239 and DFAST compliance.

- Data SLAs should be governed using a standardized template.

11

Data Sharing Agreements and Data Attestations

Data Attestations

Board of Governors of the Federal Reserve System, Proposed Revision to the FR Y-14A/Q/M effective June 30, 2016[1]

The Board of Governors of the U.S. Federal Reserve System collects information from bank holding companies (BHCs) with total consolidated assets of $50 billion or more. The Capital Assessments and Stress Testing information collection consists of the semi-annual FR Y-14A, the quarterly FR Y-14Q, and the monthly FR Y-14M reports.[2]

The FR Y-14A/Q/M reports are integral to the Federal Reserve's supervisory stress tests, as the Federal Reserve uses financial data reported by a BHC to assess whether the BHC has the capital necessary to absorb losses under stress. In previous CCAR and DFAST cycles, the Federal Reserve has found that, while respondents generally report in accordance with the instructions, material inaccuracies have been identified in reported information.

The Federal Reserve proposes to require the chief financial officer (CFO), or an equivalent senior officer (who functions as the CFO but carries a different title), of a Large Institution Supervision Coordinating Committee (LISCC) respondent to

---

[1] https://www.federalregister.gov/articles/2015/09/16/2015-23267/proposed-agency-information-collection-activities-comment-request#h-9

[2] "OMB Supporting Statement for the Capital Assessments and Stress Testing Information Collection" (FR Y-14A/Q/M; OMB No. 7100-0341), http://www.federalreserve.gov/reportforms/formsreview/FRY14A_FRY14M_FRY14Q_20151028_omb.pdf

make an attestation regarding the collection. The attestation would include two parts:

a) For projected data reported on the FR Y-14A/Q and for actual data reported on the FR Y-14A/Q/M reports, the CFO (or equivalent senior officer) of a LISCC respondent would be required to attest that the reports have been prepared in conformance with the instructions issued by the Federal Reserve System. The instructions define the scope and content of items that must be reported, and specify that the reports must be filed in accordance with U.S. generally accepted accounting principles (GAAP). The instructions further state that respondents should maintain financial records in such a manner and scope to ensure the FR Y-14A/Q/M reports reflect a fair presentation of the BHCs' financial condition and assessment of performance under stressed scenarios.

b) For actual data, the CFO (or equivalent senior officer) of a LISCC respondent would be required to attest that he or she is responsible for the internal controls over the reporting of these data, and that the data reported are materially correct to the best of his or her knowledge. The CFO would also be required to attest that the controls are effective and include those practices necessary to provide reasonable assurance as to the accuracy of these data. The CFO would be required to attest that the controls are audited annually by internal audit or compliance staff, and are assessed regularly by management of the named institution. Last, the CFO would be required to agree to report material weaknesses in these internal controls and any material errors or omissions in the data submitted to the Federal Reserve promptly as they are identified.

Data sharing agreements are contracts that govern the sharing of data between two entities. These entities may be divisions of the same company or distinct legal entities. Data sharing agreements and data SLAs have similar functionality but have key differences. Data sharing agreements are better suited to data attestations as well as enforcing acceptable use of information in downstream applications. Data SLAs are better suited to bulk movements of data.

Establish Template for Data Sharing Agreements

As discussed above, regulators will increasingly require a single executive to attest to the veracity of data in key reports. The attesting executive—such as the CFO—should require other executives—especially the Chief Risk Officer (CRO) —to certify the trustworthiness of the data being used in those reports. This approach is useful even when data attestations are not required from a regulatory perspective.

The data governance team should use a template for data sharing agreements to support data attestations, such as the example shown in Table 11.1.

Table 11.1: Template for Data Sharing Agreements	
Attribute	**Description**
Name	One-sentence description of the data sharing agreement (e.g., overall attestation on risk data by CRO to CFO)
Report	Name of the regulatory report (e.g., FR Y-14A)
Consuming executive	Name and title of executive who consumes the information (e.g., John Doe, CFO)
Producing executive	Name and title of executive who produces the information (e.g., Jill Smith, CRO)
Critical data elements	Name of the fields in the report to which the data sharing agreement applies
Effective date	Effective data of the data sharing agreement
Attestation	Certification that the data in FR Y-14A is trustworthy

Chain Multiple Data Sharing Agreements to Support Data Attestations

Data sharing agreements, and even data SLAs, can be used to manage a chained set of data attestations to support the overall data attestation to the regulators (see Figure 11.1). Each chained data sharing agreement and data SLA above is explained in Table 11.2.

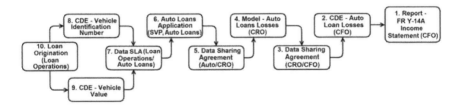

Figure 11.1: Data sharing agreements and data SLAs chained to support data attestation

Table 11.2: Chaining of Data Sharing Agreements and Data SLAs to Support Data Attestation		
Artifact	**Type**	**Attester to Report/CDE/Model/Application *or* Signatory to Data Sharing Agreement/Data SLA**
1. Federal Reserve FR Y-14A Schedule A.1.a – Income Statement	Report	CFO
2. Losses Associated with Auto Loans Held for Investment at Amortized Cost (Line Item 31 in report)	CDE	CFO
3. Sharing of auto loan risk model by CRO with CFO	Data sharing agreement	CRO (data producer) CFO (data consumer)
4. Auto loan loss risk model	Model	CRO
5. Sharing of auto loan data by auto loans division with CRO	Data sharing agreement	Senior Vice President of Auto Loans (data producer) CRO (data consumer)
6. Auto loans application	Application	Senior Vice President of Auto Loans (data executive of the auto loans data category)
7. Bulk data movement from loan origination system to auto loan application	Data SLA with acceptable thresholds for missing VINs and vehicle value	Senior Vice President of Loan Operations (data producer) Senior Vice President of Auto Loans (data consumer)
8. Vehicle Identification Number (VIN)	CDE	Senior Vice President of Loan Operations
9. Vehicle value	CDE	Senior Vice President of Loan Operations
10. Loan origination system	Application	Senior Vice President of Loan Operations

Establish Internal Controls

As discussed above, CFOs of LISCC respondents will be required to attest to the quality of internal controls. This topic is addressed in detail in Chapter 12 ("Data Governance Dashboards") and Chapter 13 ("Data Governance Audits").

Summary

- Data attestations are driven by regulatory requirements that a senior executive sign off on the veracity of data.

- Data sharing agreements are a useful tool to support data attestations.

- Data sharing agreements are contracts that govern the sharing of data between two entities.

12

Data Governance Dashboards

In Chapter 3, we discussed the formulation of data policies, standards, and processes in the form of a playbook. As part of the framework of internal controls, banks should monitor and enforce the implementation of these data policies, standards, and processes. In this chapter, we discuss the monitoring of data policies, standards, and processes based on dashboards. In Chapter 13, we will review proactive enforcement of policies, standards, and processes through data governance audits.

Establish the Data Governance Dashboard

A data governance dashboard is a useful approach to monitor compliance by relying on peer pressure to improve performance (see Table 12.1).

Table 12.1: Sample Data Governance Dashboard						
Data Policies	**Metrics**	**Enterprise Weights/ Score**	**Investment Banking**	**Corporate Banking**	**Private Banking**	**Retail Banking**
	Weight	100%	25%	25%	25%	25%
Data ownership	% data categories with data executives	33%	50%	0%	25%	75%
Metadata management	% data categories with approved CDEs	33%	25%	60%	70%	75%
Data quality management	% data categories with data quality dashboard	33%	0%	0%	25%	30%
Overall score		**36%**	**25%**	**20%**	**40%**	**60%**

A brief explanation of each field in the data governance dashboard is provided below:

- *Policy*—The dashboard covers three data policies: data ownership, metadata management, and data quality management.

- *Data governance metrics*—The dashboard covers only one metric per data policy.

- *Divisions*—The dashboard gathers metrics for investment banking, corporate banking, private banking, and retail banking.

- *Division weights*—Each division is weighted equally.

- *Metric weights*—Each metric is weighted equally.

- *Division rollup*—Each metric is scored by division. The results arc then rolled up by division: investment banking (25 percent), corporate banking (20 percent), private banking (40 percent), and retail banking (60 percent).

- *Enterprise rollup*—The division metrics are then rolled up into an enterprise metric for data governance (36 percent).

Circulate the Data Governance Dashboard on a Periodic Basis

The data governance dashboard should be generated on a monthly or quarterly basis. The dashboard must then be circulated to various stakeholders, including the data governance council, working groups, data executives, managing data stewards, and data stewards. The dashboard must be reviewed with these stakeholders to help resolve outstanding questions and to highlight key areas of improvement.

Summary

- The data governance playbook is the repository for policies, standards, and processes.

- As part of the framework of internal controls, banks should monitor and enforce the implementation of these data policies, standards, and processes.

- A data governance dashboard supports monitoring by holding data owners accountable for the implementation of policies, standards, and processes.

- The dashboard must be circulated to various stakeholders, including the data governance council, working groups, data executives, managing data stewards, and data stewards.

13

Data Governance Audits

Data governance monitoring is a softer approach to ensuring compliance with data policies, standards, and processes. On the other hand, data governance enforcement in the form of regular audits results in tangible consequences to noncompliance with data policies, standards, and processes. Regulators will have a higher level of confidence in the bank's internal controls if they observe the right level of data governance monitoring and enforcement.

Create Lines of Defense for Internal Controls

The Three Lines of Defense Model from the Committee of Sponsoring Organizations of the Treadway Commission (COSO) addresses how specific duties related to risk and control could be assigned and coordinated within an organization, regardless of its size or complexity. The model's underlying premise is that, under the oversight and direction of senior management and the board of directors, three separate groups (or *lines of defense*) within the organization are necessary for effective management of risk and control. The responsibilities of each of the lines are:[1]

- Own and manage risk and control (front-line operating management)

- Monitor risk and control in support of management (risk, control, and compliance functions put in place by management)

- Provide independent assurance to the board and senior management concerning the effectiveness of management of risk and control (internal audit)

---

[1] The Institute of Internal Auditors, Douglas J. Anderson and Gina Eubanks, *Governance and Internal Control: Leveraging COSO Across the Three Lines of Defense*, http://www.coso.org/documents/COSO-2015-3LOD-PDF.pdf

HSBC Lines of Defense

HSBC Holdings plc has implemented an activity-based "three lines of defense" model to manage operational risk.[2]

a) The first line of defense consists of every employee who is responsible for the risks that form part of their day-to-day jobs. This group owns the risks and is responsible for identifying, recording, reporting, and managing them and ensuring that the right controls and assessments are in place to mitigate these risks.

b) The second line of defense consists of global functions such as risk, finance, and human resources. This group sets the policy and guidelines for managing risks and provides advice, guidance, and challenge to the first line of defense on effective risk management.

c) The third line of defense is internal audit, which helps the board and executive management protect the assets, reputation, and sustainability of the bank. Internal audit provides independent assurance to senior management and the board over the first and second lines of defense.

Establish a Framework for Data Governance Audits

Organizations should establish a framework for data governance audits within the context of the lines of defense (see Table 13.1).

Table 13.1: Sample Framework for Data Governance Audits		
Line of Defense	**Group Conducting Data Governance Audit**	**Description**
First	Business-Unit Data Governance	Data governance audits are conducted by specific business units, such as corporate banking or investment banking, to determine compliance with policies, standards, and processes within that business unit.
	Region-Specific Data Governance	Data governance audits are conducted by a specific region, such as Asia-Pacific or Europe, to determine compliance with policies, standards, and processes within that region.

---

[2] HSBC Holdings plc, *Annual Report and Accounts 2015*

Second	Enterprise Risk Management	Data governance audits are conducted by enterprise risk management to determine compliance with policies, standards, and processes, such as model validation.
	Enterprise Data Governance	Data governance audits are conducted for specific business units, regions, and functions on a test check basis by enterprise data governance.
Third	Internal Audit	Data governance audits are conducted by internal audit.

Validate Auditability of Data Policies, Standards, and Processes in the Playbook with Internal Audit

Data governance is only enforceable if the policies, standards, and processes are auditable. Said differently, an independent party should be able to independently verify adherence to the data policies, standards, and processes that have been defined in the playbook.

The following is an example of a data standard that is not auditable:

> The company should maintain definitions of key business terms.

On the other hand, the following is an example of a data standard that is auditable:

> The data owner for each data repository is accountable to maintain a data dictionary for key business terms, column names, and table names that should be stored in the metadata repository.

Determine Evidentiary Requirements for Compliance with Data Policies, Standards, and Processes

As discussed earlier, internal audit and the data governance team must conduct periodic audits to verify compliance with policies, standards, and processes. The scope of the audit depends on the size and mission of the team that will be conducting the audit. The audit teams must clearly describe the evidentiary requirements that demonstrate adherence to data policies, standards, and processes (see Table 13.2).

Table 13.2: Evidentiary Requirements for Compliance with Data Policies, Standards, and Processes

Policy	Sample Standards	Sample Evidentiary Requirements
Data Stewardship	Ownership of data repositories	Name of data owner for the repository should be listed in the metadata repository
	Appointment of data executive for each data category	Minutes of the data governance council confirming the appointment of the data executive for each data category
	Participation by data stewards in day-to-day activities	Minutes of the working group meetings that show attendance by the data stewards
Data Architecture	Data categories should be identified	Data categories are listed in the metadata repository Minutes of the data governance council confirming the data categories
Metadata Management	CDEs should be identified for each data category	CDEs are listed with an "approved" status in the metadata repository
Data Quality Management	Data quality dashboards should be developed for each data category	Documentation to show that data quality dashboards are circulated on a periodic basis for each data category
	Data issue resolution should be implemented for each division	Documentation such as Microsoft Excel® worksheet or JIRA® to show that data issues are being triaged and resolved on a periodic basis

Manage Exceptions from Data Policies, Standards, and Processes

The data governance team must review deviations from policies, standards, and processes on an on-going basis. These deviations may be uncovered as part of regular data governance audits or in the ordinary course of business. These deviations should be reviewed at the data governance council or other appropriate forums.

Summary

- Data governance enforcement results in tangible consequences to noncompliance with policies, standards, and processes.

- The Three Lines of Defense Model is a useful framework to enforce data governance.

- Data governance audits can fit into all three lines of defense.

- Data policies, standards, and processes are enforceable only if they are auditable with clearly defined evidentiary requirements.

- Exceptions from data policies, standards, and processes must be managed tightly.

Acronyms

BCBS	Basel Committee on Banking Supervision
BHC	Bank Holding Company
BIS	Bank for International Settlements
CCAR	Comprehensive Capital Analysis and Review
CCR	Counterparty Credit Risk
CDE	Critical Data Element
CDO	Chief Data Officer
CFO	Chief Financial Officer
COSO	Committee of Sponsoring Organizations of the Treadway Commission
CPI	Consumer Price Index
CRO	Chief Risk Officer
CUSIP	Committee on Uniform Securities Identification Procedures
DAMA UK	Data Management Association, U.K. Chapter
DFAST	Dodd-Frank Act Stress Test
D-SIB	Domestic, Systemically Important Bank
EAD	Exposure at Default
ECL	Expected Credit Losses
EDM	Enterprise Data Management
EDW	Enterprise Data Warehouse

ETL	Extract Transform Load
EUC	End User Computing
FSB	Financial Stability Board
FSOC	Financial Stability Oversight Council
GAAP	Generally Accepted Accounting Principles
GDP	Gross Domestic Product
GL	General Ledger
G-SIB	Global, Systemically Important Bank
HELOC	Home Equity Line of Credit
LGD	Loss Given Default
LISCC	Large Institution Supervision Coordinating Committee
MDM	Master Data Management
NAICS	North American Industry Classification System
OCC	Office of the Comptroller of the Currency
PD	Probability of Default
PIT	Point-in-Time
RCAP	Regulatory Consistency Assessment Programme
RWA	Risk-Weighted Assets
SAR	Special Administrative Region
SIFI	Systemically Important Financial Institution
SLA	Service Level Agreement
SQL	Structured Query Language
TTC	Through-the-Cycle
VaR	Value at Risk
VIX	Market Volatility Index

B

Glossary

Acceptable threshold

The minimum level of data quality that is acceptable to business users. This metric is usually expressed as a percentage and is associated with a data quality rule. For example, if the acceptable threshold for completeness of customer IDs is 99 percent, then at least that percentage of the records should contain a customer ID that is neither null nor blank.

Accuracy

A data quality dimension relating to the degree to which data elements are accurate.

Auditability

The ability of an independent party to assess adherence of a program to predefined policies, standards, and processes.

Authoritative data source

Trusted source of data, which has been sanctioned as a source for general reuse by data architecture and data governance.

Bank Holding Company (BHC)

A company that owns and/or controls one or more U.S. banks or one that owns, or has controlling interest in, one or more banks. A bank holding company may also own another bank holding company, which in turn owns or controls a bank.[1]

---

[1] https://www.ffiec.gov/nicpubweb/Content/HELP/Institution%20Type%20Description.htm

Base attribute

A fine-grained data element such as customer first name or street name.

BCBS 239

Industry shorthand for the *Basel Committee on Banking Supervision's Principles for Effective Risk Data Aggregation and Risk Reporting*, released in January 2013.

Business glossary

Repository that contains definitions of key business terms along with relations to other artifacts, including related business terms, business rules, data quality rules, and code values.

Business lineage

Type of data lineage that provides traceability from a business perspective, including reports, models, CDEs, and data quality rules.

Calculation

The algorithm used to produce a business term.

Committee on Uniform Securities Identification Procedures (CUSIP)

A number that uniquely identifies most financial instruments, including stocks of all registered U.S. and Canadian companies, commercial paper, and U.S. government and municipal bonds.

Company-run stress test

Stress test conducted internally by a bank.

Completeness

A data quality dimension relating to the degree to which data elements are populated.

Comprehensive Capital Analysis and Review (CCAR)

Annual assessment by the U.S. Federal Reserve to evaluate a BHC's capital adequacy, capital adequacy process, and planned capital distributions, such as dividend payments and common stock repurchases.

Conformity

A data quality dimension relating to the degree to which data elements correspond to expected formats or valid values or ranges of values.

Consistency

A data quality dimension relating to the degree of relational integrity between data elements and other data elements.

Consuming executive

The executive responsible for the branch or department that uses a piece of data produced by another branch or department.

Content management

The process of digitizing, collecting, and classifying paper and electronic documents.

Credit risk

Risk that arises from the potential that a borrower or counterparty will fail to perform on an obligation.[2]

Critical data element

A data element determined to be vital to the success of an organization and/or to represent significant regulatory or operational risk; may be a base attribute or derived term, but should not constitute more than 5 to 10 percent of the total number of attributes.

Data architecture

A discipline that sets data standards for data systems as a vision or a model of the eventual interactions between those data systems.

Data attestation

A formal statement of a data set's validity and accuracy, generally performed at the executive level of an organization.

Data category

A logical classification of information to support data governance; a broad group into which data is organized in order to use it most efficiently and govern it most effectively.

Data executive

Senior leader who has ultimate responsibility for the trustworthiness of information within a data category.

---

[2] Board of Governors of the Federal Reserve System, SR 95-51 (SUP), November 14, 1995, http://www.federalreserve.gov/boarddocs/srletters/1995/sr9551.htm

Data governance

The formulation of policy to optimize, secure, and leverage information as an enterprise asset by aligning the objectives of multiple functions.

Data governance council

An enterprise-level decision-making body that sets strategy, approves the data governance playbook and funding, reviews progress, approves appointments, and manages conflicts during the data governance process.

Data governance dashboard

A data governance compliance monitoring approach, which relies on peer pressure to improve compliance.

Data governance executive

Person who is accountable for the data governance program.

Data governance executive sponsor

Person who holds ultimate accountability for the data governance program. The attesting executive for the BCBS 239 and DFAST reports is often the executive sponsor for the data governance program.

Data governance lead

Person who is accountable for leading data governance on a day-to-day basis.

Data governance monitoring

Regular reporting on the level of compliance to data policies, standards, and processes.

Data governance playbook

Guide to allow banks to establish a framework to manage data policies, standards, and processes.

Data integration

A process that involves combining data from multiple sources to provide new insights to business users.

Data lineage

The audit trail for data movement through integration processes. The result of a data lineage process is the answer to basic questions such as "Where did this data come from?" and "Where does this data go?" and "What happened to it along the way?" *See also* business lineage, technical lineage.

Data owner

The individual or role responsible for a set of data.

Data ownership

The process of identifying individuals who will be accountable for the trustworthiness of data within their purview.

Data policies

High-level goals and frameworks that set how data decisions should be made; implemented by data standards.

Data processes

Special instructions on the implementation of data standards.

Data profiling

The process of examining an existing data source's available content and collecting statistics and information about that data.

Data quality dimension

A recognized term used by data management professionals to describe a characteristic, attribute, or facet of data that can be measured or assessed against defined standards in order to determine the quality of data.[3]

Data quality management

A discipline that includes methods to measure and improve the quality and integrity of an organization's data.

Data quality scorecard

A tool to evaluate data quality; tracks key metrics by system and data domain on a regular basis.

Data Service Level Agreement (SLA)

Contracts that govern the quality, timeliness, security, and privacy of data as it moves across the enterprise between consumers and producers. Data sharing agreements and data SLAs have similar functionality but have key differences. Data sharing agreements are

---

[3] DAMA UK, *The Six Primary Dimensions for Data Quality Assessment*, October 2013.

better suited to data attestations as well as enforcing acceptable use of information in downstream applications. Data SLAs are better suited to bulk movements of data.

Data sharing agreement

Contracts that govern the sharing of data between two entities. These entities may be divisions of the same company or distinct legal entities. Data sharing agreements and data SLAs have similar functionality but have key differences. Data sharing agreements are better suited to data attestations as well as enforcing acceptable use of information in downstream applications. Data SLAs are better suited to bulk movements of data.

Data standards

The specific rules that implement data policies.

Data steward

The individual responsible for maintenance and management of data.

Derived term

A piece of data whose value is derived from the values of other data.

Dodd-Frank Act Stress Test (DFAST)

Stress testing mandated by section 165(i)(2) of the Dodd-Frank Wall Street Reform and Consumer Protection Act for all national banks and federal savings associations with total consolidated assets of more than $10 billion.

Domestic, Systemically Important Bank (D-SIB)

A bank that is not a G-SIB can still qualify as a domestic, systemically important bank (D-SIB) according to several lists maintained and released by the U.S. Federal Reserve, the European Union, or other governing bodies. D-SIB banks in the United States must comply with more stringent stress test requirements and increased supervision standards and must submit current Emergency Resolution Plans to the Federal Reserve annually.

End user computing (EUC) application

Solution that is created to meet a specific business, financial, risk management, or operational requirement and is outside the purview of the IT department.

Enterprise Data Management (EDM)

The ability of an organization to precisely define, easily integrate, and effectively retrieve data for both internal applications and external communication. It includes a number of disciplines, including data governance, data ownership, data architecture, data modeling, data integration, database management and operations, data security and privacy, master data management, reference data management, data warehousing, critical data elements, metadata management, data quality management, information lifecycle management, and content management.[4]

Euro area

The European Union member states that have adopted the euro as their common currency.

Exception ID

The unique identifier for a data quality exception in the issue tracker.

Exposure at Default (EAD)

An estimation of the extent to which a bank may be exposed to a counterparty in the event of, and at the time of, that counterparty's default.[5]

Extract Transform Load (ETL)

A process that is used in data warehousing to extract data from one or more data sources, transform the data, and load the data into a target database.

Federal Deposit Insurance Corporation (FDIC)

United States government corporation providing deposit insurance to depositors in U.S. banks.

Financial Stability Oversight Council (FSOC)

United States regulatory authority, which has a statutory mandate to identify risks and respond to emerging threats to financial stability in the United States. The FSOC is chaired by the Secretary of the

---

[4] http://en.wikipedia.org/wiki/Enterprise_data_management

[5] https://en.wikipedia.org/wiki/Exposure_at_default

U.S. Treasury and includes representatives from the Federal Reserve and other federal and state regulatory bodies.

FR Y-14A/Q/M Reports

Reports submitted by BHCs with total consolidated assets of $50 billion or more to the Board of Governors of the U.S. Federal Reserve System. The Capital Assessments and Stress Testing information collection consists of the semiannual FR Y-14A, the quarterly FR Y-14Q, and the monthly FR Y-14M reports.

Global, Systemically Important Bank (G-SIB)

Financial institution whose distress or disorderly failure, because of its size, complexity, and systemic interconnectedness, would cause significant disruption to the wider financial system and economic activity.[6] G-SIBs are subject to higher loss absorbency requirements, regular assessments of their resolvability, and higher supervisory expectations.

Impact analysis

The ability to understand how a change to one data artifact affects other data artifacts.

JIRA

Proprietary issue tracking software developed by Atlassian.

Large Institution Supervision Coordinating Committee (LISCC)

U.S. Federal Reserve System-wide committee, chaired by the director of the Board's Division of Banking Supervision and Regulation, which is tasked with overseeing the supervision of the largest, most systemically important financial institutions in the United States.

Liquidity risk

Potential that an institution will be unable to meet its obligations as they come due because of an inability to liquidate assets or obtain adequate funding (referred to as "funding liquidity risk") or that it cannot easily unwind or offset specific exposures without signifi-

---

[6] Global Financial Markets Association, http://www.gfma.org/initiatives/g-sibs/g-sibs

cantly lowering market prices because of inadequate market depth or market disruptions ("market liquidity risk").[7]

Loss Given Default (LGD)

Percentage of an exposure that is lost if a borrower defaults.

Managing data steward

Person appointed by the data executive to drive day-to-day activities. The managing data steward may own the same data categories or may own a subset of the data categories as the data executive.

Market risk

Risk of losses arising from movements in market prices. The risks subject to market risk capital charges include but are not limited to: (a) default risk, interest rate risk, credit spread risk, equity risk, foreign exchange risk, and commodities risk for trading book instruments; and (b) foreign exchange risk and commodities risk for banking book instruments.[8]

Metadata

Information that describes the characteristics of any data artifact, such as its name, location, criticality, quality, business rules, and relationships to other data artifacts.

Model validation

Process to independently validate risk models.

North American Industry Classification System (NAICS)

Standard code set used by the U.S. government to classify businesses into industries for statistical purposes.

OCC DFAST 10-50 Report

Company-run stress test, which collects detailed data on national banks and federal savings associations with consolidated assets of $10 billion to $50 billion.

---

[7] Board of Governors of the Federal Reserve System, SR 95-51 (SUP), November 14, 1995, http://www.federalreserve.gov/boarddocs/srletters/1995/sr9551.htm

[8] Basel Committee on Banking Supervision, *Minimum Capital Requirements for Market Risk*, January 2016, http://www.bis.org/bcbs/publ/d352.pdf

OCC DFAST 14A Report

Company-run stress test, which collects detailed data on covered institutions with consolidated assets of more than $50 billion.

Office of the Comptroller of the Currency (OCC)

Independent bureau of the U.S. Department of the Treasury that charters, regulates, and supervises all national banks and federal savings associations as well as federal branches and agencies of foreign banks.

Operational risk

Risk that arises from the potential that inadequate information systems, operational problems, breaches in internal controls, fraud, or unforeseen catastrophes will result in unexpected losses.[9]

Producing executive

The executive responsible for the branch or department that produces a piece of data.

Probability of Default (PD)

Financial term describing the likelihood of a default over a particular time horizon. It provides an estimate of the likelihood that a borrower will be unable to meet its debt obligations.[10]

Reference data

The defined set of values for a business term (e.g., U.S. state codes).

Related terms

The relation used to link business terms that are not synonyms or types (e.g., Real GDP and Real GDP growth are related terms).

Risk model

An assessment of financial risk to a bank, portfolio, or institution, derived from the use of formal econometric techniques.

---

[9] Board of Governors of the Federal Reserve System, SR 95-51 (SUP), November 14, 1995, http://www.federalreserve.gov/boarddocs/srletters/1995/sr9551.htm

[10] https://en.wikipedia.org/wiki/Probability_of_default

Risk-weighted assets (RWA)

A bank's assets or off-balance-sheet exposures, weighted according to risk.

Sanity check

A basic, common-sense test to evaluate whether a claim or the result of a calculation can possibly be true.

Source system

The name of the source system where a data quality check was performed.

Stress test

Process to assess the potential impact of scenarios on the consolidated earnings, losses, and capital of a covered bank over the planning horizon, taking into account the current condition of the covered bank and the covered bank's risks, exposures, strategies, and activities.[11]

Supervisory stress test

Stress test conducted by a regulator.

Synchronization

A data quality dimension relating to the degree to which data elements are consistent from one data store to the next.

Synonyms

The relation between business terms with the same definition (e.g., vendor and supplier).

Systemically Important Financial Institution (SIFI)

Financial institution including non-banking entities, such as insurance companies, whose material financial distress—or the nature, scope, size, scale, concentration, interconnectedness, or mix of its activities—could pose a threat to financial stability.[12]

---

[11] 12 CFR 325.202(l), Federal Deposit Insurance Corporation

[12] https://www.treasury.gov/initiatives/fsoc/designations/Pages/default.aspx

Technical lineage

Type of data lineage that provides traceability that includes systems, transformations, and other technical information in addition to the artifacts provided in the business lineage.

Three Lines of Defense Model

Model from the Committee of Sponsoring Organizations of the Treadway Commission (COSO) that addresses how specific duties related to risk and control could be assigned and coordinated within an organization, regardless of its size or complexity. Its underlying premise is that, under the oversight and direction of senior management and the board of directors, three separate groups (or lines of defense) within the organization are necessary for effective management of risk and control. The responsibilities of each of the lines are:[13]

a) Own and manage risk and control (front-line operating management)

b) Monitor risk and control in support of management (risk, control, and compliance functions put in place by management)

c) Provide independent assurance to the board and senior management concerning the effectiveness of management of risk and control (internal audit)

Timeliness

A data quality dimension relating to the degree to which data is available on a timely basis.

Type

A relation to show that a business term is a type of another (e.g., Seasonal GDP, Real GDP, and Nominal GDP are types of GDP. Similarly, GDP has types Seasonal GDP, Real GDP, and Nominal GDP).

---

[13] The Institute of Internal Auditors, Douglas J. Anderson and Gina Eubanks, *Governance and Internal Control: Leveraging COSO Across the Three Lines of Defense*, http://www.coso.org/documents/COSO-2015-3LOD-PDF.pdf

Uniqueness

A data quality dimension relating to the degree to which data elements are unique within a data store.

Value at Risk (VaR)

Measure of the risk of investments. It estimates how much a set of investments might lose, given normal market conditions, in a set period such as a day. VaR is typically used by firms and regulators in the financial industry to gauge the amount of assets needed to cover possible losses.[14]

---

[14] https://en.wikipedia.org/wiki/Value_at_risk

Printed in Great Britain
by Amazon